THE APOCRYPHA

DAVID A. deSILVA

Abingdon Press

Nashville

The Apocrypha

Copyright © 2012 by Abingdon Press

All rights reserved.

This book is printed on acid-free paper.

Library of Congress Cataloging-in-Publication Data has been requested.

ISBN 978-1-4267-4235-4

12 13 14 15 16 17 18 19 20 21—10 9 8 7 6 5 4 3 2 1

MANUFACTURED IN THE UNITED STATES OF AMERICA

THE APOCRYPHA

General Editors
Core Biblical Studies
Louis Stulman, *Old Testament*
Warren Carter, *New Testament*

*To James H. Charlesworth and Carl R. Holladay,
my first guides in the study of this literature*

CONTENTS

Introduction

Why Read the Apocrypha?

The label "Apocrypha" is generally given to a particular collection of Jewish writings composed between 250 BCE and 100 CE. Some of these were originally written in Hebrew or Aramaic, some were composed in Greek; all were eventually translated into Greek, the primary language in which the early Christian churches knew these texts. The texts found in the Apocrypha are only a small sampling of Jewish writings from the later Second Temple period, which would include the lengthy works of Philo of Alexandria and Flavius Josephus, several dozen parabiblical writings known as the Pseudepigrapha, and the nonbiblical texts found among the Dead Sea Scrolls.

What separates the books of the Apocrypha from all these other Jewish writings is, first and foremost, the reading practices of second- and third-century Christians, who found these books, above all other available writings, to be helpful resources alongside the books of the Jewish canon (the Christian "Old Testament") for articulating their own faith and for determining questions of ethics. The term "Apocrypha" is a transliteration of a Greek word meaning "things hidden away," and was applied to these texts in the course of debates about their status: Should they be read in public worship as Scripture, or should they be "tucked away" for private use only?[1]

The majority of the world's Christians, however, would not speak of these texts as "Apocrypha." Rather, they would speak of them as "deuterocanonical books" (a "second" canon)—or simply as part of the Old Testament. The term "deuterocanonical" does not imply a subordinate status, any more than the second commandment has less authority than the first or than Deuteronomy (the "second [giving of the] Law") falls short of the authority of the "first" statement of the Law in Exodus. Rather, it acknowledges that these texts were (generally) composed later than the books of the Hebrew Bible, such that they were excluded from the "first canon" inherited by the early church from the synagogue, and that the church only lately made a definitive pronouncement about this body of literature as canonical (at the Council of Trent in 1546), while nevertheless affirming their authority as part of the broader canon of the Catholic Church.

I have enjoyed many opportunities to talk about the Apocrypha with Christians, especially Protestant Christians, who have never read these books but are intrigued by their presence in many modern printed Bibles, including Bibles published for "ecumenical" audiences. Very often, I encounter a certain hesitation in regard to reading the Apocrypha. This hesitation is sometimes based on the presupposition that the church has weighed these books and found them to be without value, and therefore justifiably discarded and forgotten. Sometimes it is based on a prejudice that the writings included in this collection are full of false teachings that will jeopardize a reader's grasp of sound truth. Sometimes it is based just on the lingering prejudices of Protestants against Catholics—these books are in "their" Bible, and not reading them is one important thing that separates "us" from "them."

My own experience of the Apocrypha has been quite different. I was brought up in the Episcopal Church, which clearly distinguishes the apocryphal books from the Scriptures of the Old Testament, yet which also includes readings from the Apocrypha on certain Sundays and allows readings from the same for weddings and funerals. From my early teens, at least, I thought of these books as "not Scripture," but at the same time not "unscriptural"— not a threat, that is, to the scriptural witness to God, God's dealings with people, or the response from human beings for which God seeks. My experience with these texts is very much aligned with the position that I perceive the Protestant Reformers to have been recommending, and not with the position that many Protestants appear to have taken in regard to the Apocrypha since.

When Martin Luther set about translating the Bible into German, he also translated the books of the Apocrypha. While he took care to separate them out from the books of the Old Testament and to print them in a separate section, thus affirming that they were not on a level equal to that of Scripture, he still recommended them in his preface to the translation as "useful and good for reading." The degree to which Luther valued these writings is reflected above all in the fact that he took the time and the trouble to produce a German translation of the Apocrypha in the first place. This is not something one does if one's goal is to get Protestants to stop reading these books. The

English Reformers took a very similar position in regard to these texts: while they were not to be held at the same level as the canonical Scriptures, they were to be "read for example of life and instruction of manners" (article 6 of the Thirty-Nine Articles of Religion), the position that John Wesley also espoused as a priest ordained in the Anglican Church. Ulrich Zwingli and John Calvin, leaders of the Reformation in Switzerland, also took pains to provide translations of these books in their printed Bibles and to commend them for containing "much that is true and useful," though also urging caution in regard to that which "does not tend to simple truth or exact knowledge" in them.[2] In sum, then, the Apocrypha probably stand among the most important books that Protestant Christians ought to read after their canon of Scripture, and any cautions the Reformers may have issued about their use would certainly apply to the bulk of devotional literature that Christians tend to read alongside Scripture.

Why, then, should Christians of all denominations, and not just Catholic and Orthodox Christians, be concerned to read the Apocrypha?

First, the books of the Apocrypha provide important windows into the world of Second Temple period Judaism, catching us up, as it were, on a wide range of developments between the return from exile and the rebuilding of the Temple in 515 BCE and the birth of Jesus and the movement formed in his name. This range of developments extends well beyond the borders of Judea to open windows into the world of Diaspora Judaism as well—the world into which the early Christian mission quickly moved.

Books like 1 and 2 Maccabees introduce us to pivotal events in Jewish consciousness and experience, events still remembered annually in the celebration of Hanukkah. Tobit, Wisdom of Ben Sira (or Sirach), and 4 Maccabees bear witness to developments in Jewish ethical thinking and its storehouse of practical guidance. Greek Esther, Letter of Jeremiah, 3 Maccabees, and other books introduce us to the challenges of living as Jews in the Diaspora, as well as to the often strained relationships between Jews and non-Jews throughout this period and the causes thereof.

The collection as a whole allows us to peer into the ways pious Jews responded to the challenge of continuing to make traditional resources meaningful in new circumstances. Thus the apocryphal books invite us into the arena of how their authors selected, shaped, and interpreted the Jewish Scriptures—and thus contributed to the tradition of interpretation inherited by Jesus and the early church. These books give us access to theological developments that laid important foundations for early Christian theology; for example, the idea that one righteous person's death can positively influence God's relationship with others, ideas about immortality and resurrection, and ideas about the "person" of Wisdom as a being bearing God's perfect image. The Apocrypha also fill in the gaps between the worldview of the Hebrew Bible and the worldview of the New Testament, for example as witnesses to the developments in beliefs about angels and demons and their interaction with human beings.

Reading the Apocrypha is essential, then, for a more accurate picture of the faith, practices, hopes, and challenges of Jews living in the period prior to and during the ministry of Jesus and the expansion of the Christian movement (understanding "Christian" here as an alternative at the level of "Pharisaic," "Sadducean," and "Essene," not as an alternative at the level of "Jewish").

Second, many of the books of the Apocrypha contain resources available to, and used by, Jesus and his earliest disciples and apostles. The teachings of Ben Sira probably permeated the synagogues of Judea and Galilee; the story of Tobit and the teachings of its title character were similarly available throughout the land. The story of the triumph of the Maccabean heroes (both the pious martyrs and the armies of Judas) was the basis of an annual festival that Jesus, his family, and his disciples celebrated. The correspondences between Wisdom of Solomon and the writings of Paul and other members of his team are so close as to necessitate knowledge of the former on the part of the latter.

The correspondences between the teachings of Jesus and Jewish sages like Ben Sira or the author of Tobit bear witness to the greater connection between Jesus (and his followers) and the faith and practice of Judaism in the first century than is appreciated by people who "freeze" Judaism's development in the early postexilic period, such as is likely to happen for people who read only the books of the Protestant Old Testament. It would be difficult for the person who stopped studying church history before the Reformation to understand (and fairly assess) the message and mission of a John Wesley. It would be difficult for the person who stopped studying American history at the settlement of Jamestown to understand the ministry of a Martin Luther King, Jr. If we content ourselves with seeking no further information than the blank page between Malachi and Matthew, understanding Jesus in relation to the Judaism of his day will be similarly challenging.

It is true that Jesus, Paul, and the other voices speaking in the New Testament never recite a deuterocanonical text as Scripture, explicitly introducing a string of words as a quotation from Ben Sira as they do when introducing a quotation from the canonical Old Testament ("as Scripture says," "as the Holy Spirit says," "as it is written in the prophet"). This fact is probably significant for deciding what status they ascribed to the books of the Apocrypha. Nevertheless, the imprint of the teachings of these books on Jesus and the early Christian movement is undeniable. Readers who are familiar with the deuterocanonical books, then, will understand just how fully embedded Jesus, Paul, and other early Christian teachers were in the Judaism of their time, and will have a better understanding of the larger conversations to which Jesus and his followers were contributing.

Several books of the Apocrypha are also formative for early Christian theology from the earliest reflections on the preincarnate activity and existence of the Son (e.g., Col 1:15-20; Heb 1:1-4) through the formulations of the Trinity in the post-Nicene period. While the Reformers sought to curtail the use of these texts to establish new doctrines, they nevertheless had already made a significant impact upon a number of central Christian doctrines. Familiarity with at least some of the Apocrypha (especially the Wisdom of Solomon) is prerequisite to understanding the development of our own theology.

Third, the Apocrypha are rich in devotional insights, ethical admonition, and spiritually formative guidance—to such an extent that the majority of the world's Christians include them among their inspired Scriptures. The apocryphal books teach about repentance and humility before God; they give insights into the spiritual and practical disciplines required to achieve breakthroughs in personal transformation; they teach about the importance of keeping our focus on the life of eternity with God for the preservation of a life of ethical integrity. Because many of these texts were born from the struggle to discover and nurture the way of faithfulness in the midst of significant challenges, they remain devotional literature of the highest order—devotional literature that has stood the test of time and has been repeatedly affirmed by the reading practices of Catholic and Orthodox communions. Even if Protestants do not turn to these texts as sources for theological reflection, the Apocrypha can be valued as worthy and serious conversation partners in the quest for theological truth, wrestling quite openly as they do with questions of perpetual interest.

Chapter 1

What's in the Apocrypha?

A person who is familiar with the writings of the Hebrew Bible (the Protestant "Old Testament") and who embarks upon reading the Apocrypha for the first time will not find the world of these texts all that strange. There will be fresh content, to be sure, but there will also be much that is familiar. First, the deuterocanonical books are written in genres and styles that, for the most part, imitate the literature of the Hebrew Bible—the Scriptures treasured by the writers of the apocryphal books. The books that relate the history of the period are either reworked versions of canonical history books (1 Esdras) or are written in a style that closely resembles the historical books of Samuel and Kings (1 and 2 Maccabees). The Apocrypha contain collections of wisdom teachings (Sirach; the Wisdom of Solomon) that resemble the older book of Proverbs and grow organically from the broader wisdom tradition of the Hebrew Bible. The canonical book of Psalms, together with the prayers and psalms scattered throughout the Hebrew Bible, provides the model for the prayers and psalms found among the Apocrypha, whether these are independent texts (Prayer of Manasseh; Psalm 151) or embedded in longer books (Prayer of Azariah and Hymn of the Three Young Men in the Greek version of Daniel; Judith's hymn [Jdt 16]; Tobit's hymn [Tob 13]).

Second, and perhaps more important, the authors of the apocryphal books are more closely indebted to the Hebrew Bible for the content of what they write than any other source. The teachings and language of the Hebrew Bible are echoed and developed throughout this collection. The law of Moses and the covenant formed between God and the people of

1

Israel on the basis of the Law are the constant reference points throughout these texts. The explanation of the national fortunes of Israel as the history of the consequences of Israel's collective loyalty to or disloyalty against the covenant, begun in the Deuteronomistic History of 1 Samuel through 2 Kings, is accepted and adapted to the continuing history of Israel throughout the apocryphal books. The specific promises of the Old Testament prophets remain the basis for the hopes articulated by a Tobit or a Baruch; the advice of Proverbs informs the advice of Ben Sira, to the extent that later rabbis might forget what maxim comes from which source; the poetic expressions about Wisdom in the wisdom psalms and Proverbs inspire the reflections on Wisdom in Baruch, Wisdom of Solomon, and Sirach. When we read the Apocrypha, we are reading the literature of pious Jews trying to make sense of their changing circumstances in light of the unchanging revelation of their sacred texts.

In what follows, I will provide a brief text-by-text overview of the books included in the standard, expanded collection of Apocrypha as found in the New Revised Standard Version, English Standard Version, and Common English Bible translations. Unlike the books of Genesis through Nehemiah, the books of the Apocrypha are not arranged in anything like chronological order. They are also not grouped according to genre, like the books of both the Old and the New Testaments. In the survey that follows, therefore, be prepared to jump rather nimbly between Judea and the Diaspora; between the Persian, Greek, and Roman periods; and between history and fiction. The chronological, geographical, and cultural frameworks within which these books must be set will be the topic of chapter 2.

Tobit

The story of Tobit has made a significant impact on culture in the West. One can hardly find an art museum with a collection of any decent size without finding depictions of scenes from this charming story that has captivated readers for millennia. The tale was originally written in Aramaic at some point before 100 BCE, and quite probably before 200 BCE. It may have been written either in Palestine or in the eastern Diaspora (e.g., Babylon), though errors in regard to Assyrian and Babylonian geography favor Palestine, where its earliest manuscripts have also been discovered.

Tobit tells of the lives of two interrelated families living in Nineveh and Ecbatana after the exile of the northern tribes in 721 BCE. Its historical errors announce it as a work of fiction rather than an attempt at history. Tobit is a pious, charitable Jew taken into exile from Naphtali. After burying the body of a murdered fellow Jew, he takes a nap in his courtyard by the wall. The droppings of sparrows fall into his eyes and blind him, bringing him and his family into poverty. At the same time, a cousin of Tobit's is also in distress. Sarah has been married to seven men, but a jealous demon kills her husbands in the marriage chamber before they can consummate the union. God resolves to answer the prayers of both Tobit and Sarah, sending his angel Raphael to see to them.

Tobit tells his only son, Tobias, to recover a large sum of silver Tobit had deposited with a relative in faraway Media, and elicits the aid of another Jew, Azariah, to accompany him. On the way, a fish attacks Tobias while he is washing his feet, and Azariah tells him to grab it, since its inner organs can be used for healing the blind and driving away demons. Azariah leads Tobias to the home of Sarah and her parents, and arranges for their marriage, since Tobias is her relative. Tobias burns the fish's liver and heart to drive away the demon, and Sarah's family is overjoyed. Azariah proceeds to Media to collect the silver while the couple celebrates the wedding feast, then returns with Tobias and Sarah to Nineveh, where Tobias smears the fish's gall on Tobit's eyes and heals them. Azariah reveals to Tobit and Tobias that he is an archangel of God, sent to heal them on account of Tobit's many acts of charity. Tobit concludes with a hymn and, finally, his deathbed instructions to his son.

This book is a vital witness to the ethics of Diaspora Jews, especially emphasizing almsgiving and other works of charity, the importance of marrying within the Jewish family, and the value of kinship relations. It also bears witness to the theological developments of the period, including angelology and demonology, the affirmation of Deuteronomy's interpretation of national prosperity and misfortune (extending this to individuals), the explanation of individual suffering as a test of faithfulness (as in Job), and the eschatological restoration and exaltation of Jerusalem.

> They praised the God of heaven, saying, "Blessed are you, God, with every pure blessing; may people bless you forever! Blessed are you, because you have brought me joy. It didn't happen as I had expected. Instead, you have dealt with us according to your great mercy. (Tob 8:15-16)

3

Judith

Judith is another work of historical fiction without pretensions to representing a "true" history. For example, Judith 5:18-19 relates the destruction of Jerusalem and its Temple as past history even though, in the world of the story, Nebuchadnezzar was only now threatening to do this very thing. The story reflects some of the dynamics of the Maccabean Revolution, and may well have been written in Judea at some point during the Hasmonean dynasty, the brief window of independence enjoyed by Judea after the revolution (142–63 BCE).

After his western allies refuse to obey Nebuchadnezzar's summons to aid him in a war, he vows to avenge his honor by subjugating the disobedient lands one by one and destroying their sacred shrines. His general, Holofernes, finally makes his way to Judea where he besieges Bethulia as a fortress town positioned for the strategic defense of Jerusalem. Their stores and water nearly depleted, the elders of Bethulia promise to hand over the city in five days if God has not by then delivered them. Judith, a beautiful and pious widow, now emerges as the heroine who promises to liberate her city. She goes to Holofernes's camp, pretending to flee the coming destruction of her city. She claims that they have violated God's Law by planning to eat the foods set apart for the tithe, and that God will show her when this transgression transpires so that Holofernes can attack them with no fear of divine intervention. She is welcomed into the camp and praised for her wisdom in defecting. She leaves the camp nightly, ostensibly to pray for this revelation. On the fourth night, she allows Holofernes to believe that she is succumbing to his advances and encourages him to drink too much. Once alone with him in his tent, she cuts off the stupefied Holofernes's head with his own sword and escapes from the camp, having established her routine of nightly prayer.

Although featuring a female heroine and thus the potential and value of a "good woman," the book also bears witness to the persistence of traditional values concerning women; that is, to be killed by the hand of a woman, the weakest enemy, is the greatest disgrace. There is no virtue for women when their chastity has been compromised. Even though Judith can emerge as a heroine in a time of crisis, her proper place remains outside the male sphere of governance. The book of Judith remains a rich witness to the theology and ethics of the period, as well as the surprising (and disturbing) use of deceit as a laudable means to defeat an enemy of one's people.

> Look at their arrogance, and send your wrath upon their heads. Give my hand, the hand of a widow, the strength to do what I have planned. By using my lying lips, strike down the slave along with the ruler, the ruler along with his servant. Break their pride by the hand of a woman. (Jdt 9:9-10)

Esther (Greek)

The book of Esther had some difficulty gaining canonical status both in the synagogue (its status was apparently still being disputed in the late first century CE) and in the early church. In part, this may have been due to the fact that, in its original Hebrew form, it is hardly a religious text. To the extent that God appears, God is at work well behind the scenes—an assumed agent and not a leading player. The situation is quite different with the version of Esther as it existed in Greek translations at the turn of the era. This version contains six substantial additions (in older English translations, these are often separated out as the "Additions to Esther") as well as many minor changes throughout the text. These changes and additions introduce a strongly theological element that was strangely lacking in the Hebrew version.

Greek Esther opens with a report of a dream vision that Mordecai experiences, the meaning of which becomes clear at the end of the book (giving the whole book a religious frame). Another lengthy addition presents the prayers offered by Mordecai and by Esther prior to the latter's entrance before the king to set in motion her people's deliverance. In her prayer, "Esther" explains her crossing of unacceptable boundaries (e.g., marrying the Gentile king, eating with Gentiles, and possibly participating in the worship of the king's gods), affirming that she has never eaten forbidden food, participated in idol worship, or enjoyed sharing a bed with an uncircumcised male. God intervenes directly in another addition, turning the king's anger into compassion and concern for Esther. Two further additions expand the texts of the edict against Jews and the edict rescinding the former action, providing windows into ancient anti-Judaism. Throughout Greek Esther, the boundary between Jew and Gentile is dramatically reaffirmed in God's providential care for the former, but not for the latter.

God has done signs and great wonders that have not happened among the nations. For this reason God made two lots, one to represent God's people and one to represent the nations. These two lots came before God for the hour and season and day of decision in the presence of all the nations. God remembered his people and affirmed the just cause of his inheritance. (Gk Esth 10:6-9)

Wisdom of Solomon

Solomon was the quintessential sage in Israelite tradition, and so it is not surprising to find anonymous sages continuing to attribute their writings to the patron saint of Jewish wisdom. The so-called Wisdom of Solomon was composed in Greek, judging from the author's use of the Greek translation of the Jewish Scriptures and from his use of compositional techniques that are native to Greek writing, during the early Roman imperial period. It is also likely that he wrote in Egypt, perhaps from the major Jewish Diaspora community of Alexandria, given the special animosity toward Egyptians reflected in the book and the special interest in criticizing the worship of animals, a common feature of Egyptian religion.

Unlike Proverbs, essentially a collection of two-line maxims with little or no relationship to one another, Wisdom of Solomon offers well-developed reflections on just a few key topics. The author offers an essay on how living only for the life of this world perverts human ethics and relationships, but how God will vindicate beyond death those who remain committed to live righteously before God and do not relinquish their hope in God. Writing unmistakably in the persona of Solomon, he then writes about the nature of Wisdom and her role in creation and in the life of the pious. The final third of the book is essentially a sermon on the plagues of Exodus, stressing God's providential care for God's people and punishment of their enemies, and including a lengthy examination of the folly of Gentile religion (including the ruler cult).

Together with Sirach, this was no doubt one of the most influential and important of the apocryphal books in the early church and in the formation of Christian doctrine.

> Who's ever known your counsel, unless you gave them wisdom and sent down your Holy Spirit from on high? Only then did your ways become clear to us on earth. Only then were humans able to learn what pleases you, and were thus rescued by wisdom. (Wis 9:17-18)

Wisdom of Ben Sira (Sirach)

Yeshua ben Sira was a scribe and a sage who directed a school in Jerusalem in the first quarter of the second century BCE, presumably for the education of the youth of the elite, both priestly and lay, for a variety of careers. The book bearing his name preserves a compendium of his instructions across a broad spectrum of topics. Ben Sira wrote in Hebrew, and about one-third of his original has been recovered. We are, in the main, dependent upon the Greek translation undertaken by his grandson, who sought to make his grandfather's wisdom available to Jews living in Hellenistic Egypt.

Ben Sira lived during a period in which Jerusalem and its elite were being drawn toward adapting to the essentially Greek culture of the ruling powers (both in Egypt and in Syria) for the sake of greater acceptance by and closer involvement with the dominant culture. Ben Sira himself benefits in many ways from the spread of Hellenistic culture, not least in what he has learned from Egyptian sages in regard to wisdom in politics and from Greek sages in regard to practical advice in areas such as choosing confidants, conducting oneself properly toward friends, and guarding one's speech. However, he taught his students to resist the tendencies toward assimilation to the Greek culture wherever this threatened diligent observance of the Torah, which for him remained the irreplaceable source of personal honor and national security, seen especially in his praise of Jewish heroes and censure of those who led Israel away from covenant loyalty. Far from being a burden or a manifestation of legalism, Torah was celebrated as God's special gift to Israel, God's gracing of Israel, a view that reverberates throughout the Apocrypha.

Alongside this general concern running throughout his work, Ben Sira left behind a valuable body of reflections on providence and free will, prayer, temptation, forgiveness, and almsgiving, as well as the practical advice on how to succeed in "society" that his students expected. He thus provides important windows into social practices and relationships, such as the expectations of friends and patrons, management of the ancient household, proper behavior at symposia (drinking parties), and the dangers that must be navigated by the player in politics. One area in which Ben Sira is justly criticized is his view of women as essentially a liability to a man's honor and peace of mind, in which he tends to go even beyond the norms of his culture. Much of his material concerning women, however, does bear witness to the broader elevation of silence, submissiveness, and chastity as primary values to be nurtured by women in his world.

> Fearing the Lord is the whole of wisdom,
>   and all wisdom involves doing the Law. . . .
> Someone who fears God but who has inferior intelligence
>   is better than someone who abounds in intelligence
> but who violates the Law.
> (Sir 19:20, 24)

Baruch

Baruch was Jeremiah's scribe and, thus, an important figure in the prophet's ministry. As a writer working in the shadow of a prophet, and thus of the prophetic spirit, the person of Baruch attracted the attention of later authors in the Second Temple period who chose to write their own works in Baruch's name, beginning with this text. Baruch opens with a scene of public, corporate repentance on the part of the exiled Judean community in Babylon, which sends money for offerings to be made in Jerusalem and prescribes a litany of repentance to be spoken on behalf of the Jews in Judea and the Diaspora. This first half of the book may have been authored in Hebrew anytime during the third or second century BCE. The confession of sin and plea for forgiveness are now followed by a wisdom poem reminiscent of the language of Job 28:12-28 and Deuteronomy 30:15-19, directing the reader to the keeping of Torah, which is Wisdom itself, as the path to national recovery. The last segment of Baruch takes on a more prophetic style, first expressing a lament spoken, as it were, by Jerusalem over her children, and then articulating afresh the prophetic message of hope for the restoration of Jerusalem and its inhabitants, especially as found in Isaiah 49–62. The second half may have been composed in Greek somewhat later than the first half (perhaps as recently as the late first century BCE). While some might criticize Baruch for its lack of originality, its authors have composed a highly effective summary of the scriptural tradition as it pertains to Jewish life under Gentile domination.

> Turn your anger away from us, for only a few of us remain among the nations where you have scattered us. Lord, listen to our prayer and our pleading. For your own sake, set us free and give us favor with those who have brought us into exile so that all the earth might know that you are the Lord our God, since Israel and her children carry your name. (Bar 2:13-15)

Letter of Jeremiah

Closely associated with the book of Baruch (to the point that, in older Bibles, it is simply presented as the sixth chapter of the same book) is a letter written as if by Jeremiah to the first exiles being deported to Babylon. The actual author, however, addresses fellow Jews in every location, surrounded as they are by Gentiles practicing—sometimes quite fervently—the cults of their gods around the images of the same. Drawing on older prophetic tirades against idols (especially Isa 46:6-7; Jer 10:2-15), the author stresses the manufactured, artificial nature of the Gentiles' gods as represented by the idols themselves. Since these idols can't see, hear, speak, dress themselves, pick themselves up when they fall over, or otherwise protect themselves from animals and thieves, the Gentiles' "gods" are empty and their religion a joke. Punctuating the letter are two refrains: "Clearly they are no gods, so don't be afraid of them" (Let Jer 14; see, similarly, vv. 22, 28, 64, 68); and "So why should anyone consider or call them gods?" (v. 39; see, similarly, vv. 44, 56, 63).

The letter doesn't adequately engage Gentile religion (since Gentiles themselves would say that the lifeless idol was not their god, but merely a representation), but its main aim was to help insulate other Jews from being impressed by and drawn to the cults of the majority around them, particularly the Jews living in Diaspora communities in Gentile lands. The Hebrew original may date back to the late fourth century BCE, and thus represent one of the earliest texts in the collection.

> Be careful that you don't become like the Gentiles, letting fear of these gods grip you, especially when you see large crowds of people walking in front of and behind them, worshipping them. But say to yourself, Lord, we want to worship you. (Let Jer 4-5)

9

Additions to Greek Daniel

The book of Daniel, as it was known in its Greek form, was considerably longer than the earlier Hebrew and Aramaic version of the book. Sometime after its composition or compilation in what Jews and Protestants would call its canonical form (Dan 1–12), it was expanded to include two additional court stories and several liturgical pieces—the stories of Susanna and of Daniel's encounters with Bel and the Snake (or the Dragon), and the Prayer of Azariah and the Hymn of the Three Young Men. These four additions were composed prior to 100 BCE, the time of the translation of Daniel into Greek; some of these additions might predate the final form of Hebrew-Aramaic Daniel.

The story of the three young men cast into the furnace in Daniel 3 inspired the composition and introduction of two liturgical texts into the narrative. An anonymous author crafted a beautiful corporate confession of sin and plea for deliverance, placing this on the lips of Azariah in the furnace. He affirms God's justice in all that has happened to Israel, confesses Israel's sins and expresses deep sorrow, and begs God to vindicate God's people for the sake of God's own honor among the nations, since this is tied to God's people's survival or destruction. After God's angel intervenes to create a space of coolness within the furnace for the three loyal Jews, they sing a hymn praising God for his deliverance and calling upon the entire created order—heavenly and meteorological phenomena, earthly phenomena and beings, and finally human beings—to join in God's praise.

> In this time we have no ruler or prophet or leader,
>   no entirely burned offering or sacrifice, no special gift or incense,
>   no place to bring gifts to you and find mercy.
> Accept us, please, with our crushed souls and humble spirits,
>   as if we brought entirely burned offerings of rams and bulls,
>   as if we brought tens of thousands of fat lambs. (Pr Azar 15-16)

The tale of Susanna glorifies the wisdom of the young Daniel, who is able to prevent a gross miscarriage of justice. Two elders, entrusted with oversight of the Jewish community in exile in Babylon, conspire to entrap a young wife into consenting to commit adultery with them. She chooses to resist them rather than violate God's Law, and they claim to have caught her in the act of adultery with a young man who fled the scene. On their testimony, Susanna is condemned to death. At this point, Daniel jumps up and exclaims her innocence. He cross-examines the elders individually, catches them in a point of disagreement in their testimonies, and demonstrates them to have borne false witness. Susanna is spared, and the elders are executed.

> Susanna groaned. "I'm trapped! If I do this, it's death; but if I don't, I still won't escape your plotting. But I'd rather not do this and fall into your hands, than sin in the Lord's sight." (Sus 22-23)

The story of Susanna sometimes appears at the beginning of Daniel, introducing him thus as a wise and spirit-inspired young man. In other Greek manuscripts, Susanna follows Daniel 12. Greek Daniel is consistently closed, however, with the story of an older Daniel successfully unmasking the lies perpetrated upon followers of two local cults. Cyrus the king asks Daniel why he does not worship Bel, when the idol itself consumes the food and wine left out for it each night. Daniel reveals (by secretly spreading ashes upon the floor of the temple) that it is the priests of Bel and their families who sneak into the temple each night and consume the food, making Bel look like a "living" God. Cyrus brings Daniel to the cult site of a giant snake, which Daniel surely cannot dispute is a living god. Daniel acknowledges that the animal is living, but he is able to kill it by feeding it cakes of pitch, fat, and hair, proving that it is no god. The citizens insist that Daniel be thrown to the lions for desecrating their cults, but Daniel is miraculously delivered, to Cyrus's delight.

> The king honored Bel and worshipped it daily, but Daniel worshipped his own God. So the king said to him, "Why don't you worship Bel?" He said, "I don't honor idols made by humans, rather the living God who created heaven and earth and has authority over all living things." (Bel 4-5)

11

These stories make the book of Daniel even more relevant for Diaspora Jews than the Hebrew-Aramaic original, dealing with the ever-present issue of Gentile cults and the need to insulate Jews against the power of the religion of the majority, and with the dangers even within the local Jewish community when sin subverts commitment to justice and covenant loyalty.

1 and 2 Maccabees

Unlike 1 and 2 Samuel or 1 and 2 Kings, which represent successive installments in the story of Israel's monarchy, 1 and 2 Maccabees both tell essentially the same story, but from different angles and with different emphases. This is the story of an attempt to transform Jerusalem into a Greek city and to make Judea more fully a part of the larger Greek world, the violent suppression of traditional Judaism, and the successful resistance on the part of faithful Jews.

The book of 1 Maccabees is most interested in the actions of Judas Maccabeus and his brothers, telling the story of their successful revolution against Greco-Syrian rule and their establishing of a new hereditary dynasty over Israel. The author seems most intent to promote their rule as legitimate—the family's fitting reward for its personal investment in the good of Judea.

> "How should we thank Simon and his sons? He and his brothers, and his father's family, have stood firm. They have fought and repelled Israel's enemies and established our freedom." . . . So they made him their leader and high priest, because he had done all these things and had acted toward his nation with justice and loyalty. He sought in every way to lift up his people. (1 Macc 14:25-26, 35)

The book of 2 Maccabees, while still glorifying Judas, gives more of a theological interpretation to events, using the history to underscore the ongoing validity of the blessings and curses set down in Deuteronomy. As long as Judeans keep the covenant, their lives remain stable and secure under God's protection. Initiatives to break the covenant to become more like the Gentile nations result in national disaster. Second Maccabees is also much more interested in the internal intrigues among the Jews leading up to the

Hellenizing Crisis and in another kind of hero—the faithful, courageous martyrs who faced down a tyrant and, through their obedience unto death, reconciled the people to God and allowed Judas and his brothers to enjoy success in battle.

Both histories record the story of the recovery and cleansing of the Jerusalem Temple from the "abomination of desolation" (the "digusting and destructive thing" in the CEB) and the institution of an annual festival to remember God's deliverance of God's own holy place—still remembered each winter in Hanukkah.

> The Maccabee and his companions, with the Lord leading them, recovered the temple and the city. . . . On the anniversary of the temple's defilement by foreigners, on that very day, the sanctuary was purified, on the twenty-fifth of the month, which is Kislev. . . . So they held ivy wands, beautiful branches, and also palm leaves, and offered hymns to the one who had made the purification of his own temple possible. They voted and issued a public decree that all Jews should celebrate these days each year. (2 Macc 10:1, 5, 7-8)

1 Esdras

First Esdras presents an alternative version of the story found in 2 Chronicles 35–36, Ezra, and Nehemiah 8, though its ending has been lost (and perhaps its original opening as well). It was probably originally composed in Hebrew or Aramaic in the second or first century BCE. Like its canonical counterpart, 1 Esdras stresses the importance of genealogy for belonging to Israel and for knowing one's place within Israel. Only priests and Levites whose genealogies are "on record" can serve in the restored Temple. Only genealogical descent from Israel qualifies one to be part of Israel. This last point is dramatized when Ezra calls upon the congregation of those who had returned from the Babylonian exile in the waves before his arrival to dismiss their "foreign" wives and disown the mixed offspring produced from these unions, so that the holy race might remain pure.

What most sets 1 Esdras apart from canonical Ezra and Nehemiah is the former's inclusion of the "Contest of the Bodyguards." Three of King Darius's bodyguards devise a challenge among themselves: Who can provide the most thoughtful answer to the question "What is strongest?" The three bodyguards write down the question and their answers, and place them under the king's pillow. The next day, the king invites each to explain. The first offers that wine is the strongest power, since it clouds the minds of people. The second suggests that men are strongest, and, of these, the strongest is the king. The third answers that women are stronger still, since even the king's concubine can bend the king to her will, but that the strongest thing in the cosmos is truth. The king rewards the third bodyguard for the best answer.

The author of 1 Esdras incorporates this preexisting tale and names its hero Zerubbabel, who then asks for the favor of returning to Jerusalem and getting the repairs to the Temple and city back on track. It is clear from the author's rearrangement of the whole, and his incorporation of this otherwise gratuitous court tale, that he is driven by a desire to elevate Zerubbabel in his version of the history—to the point that Zerubbabel absorbs the functions of Nehemiah, who plays no role here. The author may have set out to give a sense that David's throne had been restored, and thus that God's promises to David had been fulfilled in Zerubbabel, even though the latter was not officially a king.

> You, Lord, removed our sins, and you gave us such a root as this. Yet we again turned away to disobey your Law by intermixing with the impure of the neighboring peoples. Weren't you angry enough with us to destroy us without leaving a root or a descendant or our honor?
>
> Lord of Israel, you are true. We are left as a root this very day.
> (1 Esd 8:84-86)

Prayer of Manasseh

Manasseh was the most wicked king of Judah. His sins against God were so great that nothing could avert the catastrophic judgment against Jerusalem to come (2 Kgs 21:2-15; 24:1-4), not even the pious reforms undertaken by Josiah (2 Kgs 23:26-27). He is remembered more benignly in 2 Chronicles, however. After he was taken into captivity, Manasseh repented of his sins and returned to Judah a changed and pious king. The Chronicler writes that his prayer is recorded in the long-lost "records of Israel's kings" and "the records of Hozai [or, the seers]" (2 Chr 33:18-19). A Jewish poet, therefore, re-created this lost prayer, giving expression to the boundless mercies of God

14

in a penitential psalm that continues to be prayed in Christian churches. The original language (whether Hebrew or Greek) and the time of its composition are not certain.

> You, Lord, are the God of those who turn from their sins.
> In me you'll show how kind you are.
>   Although I'm not worthy, you'll save me according
>   to your great mercy.
> I will praise you continuously all the days of my life. (Pr Man 13-15)

Psalm 151

Many biblical psalms are connected with events in the life of David, for example the prayer of repentance linked with his conviction by Nathan for having seduced Bathsheba and orchestrated the death of Uriah in battle (Ps 51). Yet no psalms commemorate two of the most significant events in David's life—his anointing as king by Samuel and his defeat of Goliath (1 Sam 16–17). Two anonymous poets therefore composed psalms celebrating these events, echoing the biblical stories at several points. These psalms were preserved in the original Hebrew in the Psalms scroll found among the Dead Sea Scrolls (which contained several additional psalms and prayers besides). While these were originally separate compositions, the psalm concerned with the anointing of David was later abbreviated and joined to the psalm celebrating his victory over Goliath, perhaps in the course of their translation from Hebrew into Greek.

Many motives could urge a poet to create such hymns, but why would Jews read, recite, and preserve them? It may be that David's story spoke directly to their situation of being relatively small and unimpressive in the midst of greater powers, even in the midst of giants. God's choice of David, in part motivated by David's worship of the One God, and David's victory over Goliath may have given assurance to the people of Judea that God still chooses the weak and even gives them victory over far superior forces, such as those still surrounding them.

15

3 Maccabees

The book of 3 Maccabees is a work of historical fiction written by a Jew in Egypt, quite probably from within the large Jewish community in Alexandria. Its date is uncertain, but the likeliest theories place it in the early Roman period, from the time of either Augustus (31 BCE–14 CE) or Caligula (37–41 CE). The title is misleading, since the story it tells unfolds in Egypt fifty years before the Maccabean Revolt. The king of Egypt, Ptolemy IV, defeats the king of Syria and Babylon, Antiochus III, in a battle at Raphia. After this, he visits the major cities of his kingdom to encourage the population and honor their shrines. When he is not allowed to enter the shrine in Jerusalem, he is enraged and returns to Alexandria determined that the Jews in the heartland of his empire will either convert to a more inclusive religion or be killed. Only a few Jews accept the king's invitation to participate in pagan rites and to be enfranchised as citizens of Alexandria. The vast majority are therefore herded together into the hippodrome outside the city to be trampled by war elephants. God responds to the prayers of God's people, however, and miraculously rescues the loyal Jews from certain death. Ptolemy allows the faithful to punish the apostate Jews and provides all that is needed for a seven-day festival, which is to become an annual observance in honor of God's deliverance.

The story very closely parallels the history told in 2 Maccabees, from an assault on the Jerusalem Temple to a violent suppression of the Jewish way of life to the establishment and promotion of a festival commemorating God's deliverance, which may account for the book's grouping among the "Books of the Maccabees." The story affirms that Jews in the Diaspora, just like Jews in Judea, are bound to the fate of the Temple and that God is present to hear and save God's people whether or not they are in the land of promise. While it is, in the main, unhistorical (there was a battle of Raphia; there was an attempt to register Jews for a poll tax under Augustus; there were anti-Jewish actions taken by Ptolemy VIII, though for very different reasons), the book of 3 Maccabees bears a useful witness to the tensions between Jews and non-Jews in the Greek world as well as to the challenges Jews faced living in a land not their own.

> Let it be shown to all the Gentiles that you are with us, Lord, and you haven't turned your face away from us. But just as you have said, "Not even when they were in the land of their enemies did I neglect them," so bring it to pass, Lord. (3 Macc 6:15)

2 Esdras

The Apocrypha includes one example of the genre of apocalypse, a kind of literature familiar from Daniel 7–12 and Revelation. Apocalypses generally involve revelations of the spaces not normally accessible to human beings (the heavenly and infernal realms) and times beyond the present (the primeval past and the eschatological future), the effect of which is to shine an interpretive light on the present space and time of the author and the audience, putting its challenges in a larger, God-centered perspective.

The book of 2 Esdras is actually a composite work. The core (2 Esd 3–14, now often referred to as 4 Ezra) is a Jewish apocalypse written at the end of the first century CE. Its author wrestles with the big questions of his day concerning God's providence and justice. What good did it do Israel for God to give it the Law without removing the sinful inclination to disobey God's Law? What does it mean to be God's "chosen people" when Judea is trampled by the empire of Rome, which doesn't give God a second thought and yet continues to prosper? "Ezra's" conversation partner, the angel Uriel, points him to two solutions. The first is found beyond death, when God will reward the pious and punish those who failed in life's greatest contest, namely fighting against the evil inclination and obeying Torah. The second is found in the eschatological future when God's Messiah will indict Rome (presented as a many-headed, many-winged eagle) for its crimes and usher in an age of peace. In a final episode, God restores through Ezra the inspired text of the twenty-four books of the Hebrew Scriptures as well as the text of a much broader number of books to be reserved for use by only the wise (though strikingly inspired by the same source).

The prologue (2 Esd 1–2, often called 5 Ezra) is a Christian addition from the second century. In it, God accuses Israel of ingratitude for God's countless mercies and promises the kingdom to another people. Fifth Ezra shows clear dependence on Matthew and Revelation in its vision of the redeemed standing before God's Son. The epilogue (2 Esd 15–16, also known as 6 Ezra) is a separate Christian addition from the third century, taking the form of a prophetic denunciation of Rome and the provinces in league with Rome during a period of persecution.

> You have said that the other nations born of Adam are nothing, that they are like spit, and you have compared their abundance to a drop from a pitcher. But look now, Lord! These nations that are valued as nothing rule over us and devour us, while we, your people, . . . your dearest ones, are handed over to them. If the world was created for our sake, why don't we possess our world as an inheritance? How long will this situation last? (2 Esd 6:56-59)

4 Maccabees

The last book in the collection was composed in excellent Greek, probably in the southern region of Asia Minor, and probably during the middle half of the first century CE. The author presents his speech as an oration on the topic that "God-centered thinking is supreme over emotions and desires" (4 Macc 1:1, author's translation), and thus as a contribution to a very popular and important theme in Greek and Latin philosophical ethics, namely the "mastery of the passions" that get in the way of living virtuously. His driving point, however, is that the Jewish Torah is the best possible training program for the mastery of one's cravings, desires, and feelings. He seeks to prove this by discussing how particular laws curtail particular vices and drives and by appealing briefly to the examples of Joseph, Moses, and David. The largest part of his speech (3:19–18:24), however, focuses on the example of the pious Jews martyred during the Hellenizing Crisis of 168–166 BCE—the aged priest Eleazar, seven young brothers, and the mother of the seven—as his strongest proofs (hence the title, appropriately linking this book with the other books of the "Maccabees"). Their understanding of their personal debt to the Creator God and of the greater rewards and dangers associated with fulfilling or not fulfilling that debt enables them to withstand the sharpest emotions (fear, watching loved ones suffer and die) and the fiercest physical agonies—proof that the Torah-instructed person has the greatest capacity for persevering in virtue.

The author's mastery of Greek composition and rhetoric, his familiarity with Greek philosophical debates about the mastery of the passions, his awareness of other Greek ethical conversations (such as the characteristics of the wise, free person; the nature of brotherly and sisterly love; and the nature of love for offspring), and his familiarity even with conventions of Greek tragedy show how fully "hellenized" a Jew could be without sacrificing commitment to, and observance of, the Torah and its distinctive way of life in all its particulars.

> When God formed human beings, God planted emotions and character traits inside them. At that time, God also set the mind on the throne in the middle of the senses, to function as a holy governor over them all. God gave the Law to the mind. Whoever lives in line with the Law will rule over a kingdom that is self-controlled, just, good, and courageous. (4 Macc 2:21-23)

Chapter 2

The World of the
Apocrypha

The last phase of the history related in the Hebrew Bible concerns events following the conquest of Babylon by Cyrus of Persia in 539 BCE. Cyrus allowed resettled exiles to return to their native lands, including the Judean exiles, whom he authorized to restore their capital city and their Temple. Work on the latter—the rebuilt, hence "Second" Temple—was completed around 515 BCE. Work on the former was completed only under Nehemiah's governorship in the years following 445 BCE. Nothing more is said of Israelite history in the Protestant Bible until Herod rules over Judea under the supervision of Augustus (Matt 2:1; Luke 1:5).

Several books among the Apocrypha fill in important gaps in this history, chiefly in regard to the end of the period of Greek domination and the early period of the briefly renewed Judean independence. First and Second Maccabees are essential sources in this regard. Second Maccabees is a condensed version of a five-scroll-long history of the Maccabean Revolt by Jason of Cyrene, who may have been a contemporary of these events. It introduces us to the inner-Judean intrigues leading up to the Hellenizing Crisis, as well as giving an account of the early years of the Maccabean Revolt, thus covering 175–161 BCE. First Maccabees is concerned mostly with the revolt itself and with the founding of the Hasmonean dynasty, covering 167–141 BCE.[1] The visions in Daniel 7–12 also focus primarily upon the history of the intertestamental period down to about 166 BCE, with the result that familiarity with this story greatly helps us to understand that text as well. The history of the tumultuous years between 175 and 164 BCE are of special importance for the formation of Jewish consciousness in the time of Jesus, since these events were remembered annually in the Festival of Hanukkah (or "Dedication," John 10:22).

For the fuller picture of this period, we rely on the first-century CE Jewish historian Flavius Josephus, especially books 12–14 of his *Antiquities* and the opening sections of his *Jewish War*. Greek and Latin historians provide the larger historical framework of the actions of the Seleucids and Ptolemies against each other and in regard to the West, within which the events related in 1 Maccabees, 2 Maccabees, and Daniel 7–12 fit.[2]

Judea Under Hellenistic Rule

Alexander the Great brought an end to the "Persian period" in Judea as he began to carry out his own plans for imperial expansion in 334–331 BCE, taking Asia Minor, Syria, Palestine, and Egypt away from the Persian king Darius III (1 Macc 1:1-4; Dan 8:3-7, 19-21; 11:2-3). Eventually he would push eastward into Babylonia as far as the Indus River. In 323 BCE, at the height of his power, Alexander died of a fever, leaving no viable heir. His empire was quickly divided among his chief generals (the Diadochoi or "successors"), who would battle with one another for more than twenty years until the surviving generals settled upon a four-way division of the territory after the battle of Ipsus in 301 BCE (1 Macc 1:5-8; Dan 8:8, 21-22; 11:3-4). The most important of these generals-turned-kings for Judean history are Ptolemy I Soter (322–285 BCE), who held Egypt and Palestine (the first "king of the South," in the language of Dan 11:5 NRSV), and Seleucus I Nicator (312–280 BCE), who held Syria and Babylonia (the first "king of the north," Dan 11:6 NRSV).[3] Possession of Palestine would be a point of contention between these dynasties for the next century and a half. The treaty following the battle of Ipsus actually awarded Palestine to Seleucus I, though Ptolemy I did not relinquish his hold upon it (an issue that Seleucus I did not press, since he owed his position, in part at least, to Ptolemy). His successors, however, did press their claim. Daniel's summary of the history of the descendants of Ptolemy and Seleucus as an alternation between invasions of one another's territory and uneasy truces is quite accurate (Dan 2:41-43; 11:6-16).

The descendants of Ptolemy I maintained their hold on Judea through 198 BCE. Antiochus III ("the Great," 226–187 BCE) twice attempted to take Palestine from Ptolemaic control. Though his first campaign ended in failure at the battle of Raphia (217 BCE; Dan 11:10-11; 3 Macc 1:1-5), his second campaign succeeded brilliantly (Dan 11:13-16). Antiochus III continued the Ptolemies' policy of allowing the Judeans to govern themselves in accordance with their ancestral law (the Torah, the law of Moses), and made generous allowances for tax relief for several years while the land recovered from the many battles that had been fought upon it.

Antiochus III set his sights on claiming the coastlands of Asia Minor and even Greece itself for his empire, but Rome, the great power to the west, halted his efforts at any western expansion as a threat to their own interests in the East. The Roman navy defeated his fleet, and, a few years later, their armies defeated his forces at Magnesia in 190 BCE. Rome imposed a treaty that would severely limit Seleucid initiatives. It also imposed a heavy financial penalty for "war reparations"—the heaviest ever to be imposed in the ancient world—and an annual tribute to Rome. This fiscal burden would play a large part in Seleucid policy in Judea and other territories in the years to come. Antiochus III would, in fact, die while attempting to confiscate the money deposited in a temple of Bel in Elymaïs in 187 BCE (Dan 11:18-19), motivated by his debt to Rome and his own expenses incurred in an unsuccessful war in Asia Minor and Greece.

During this period, Judea, like all territories within Alexander's empire and the empires of his successors, was drawn into a process of "hellenization." This process involved the dissemination of Greek language, culture, and political practices as Macedonians and Greeks found themselves relocated across this wide expanse of territory and as local elites tried to maintain their positions by assimilating themselves to their conquerors. Native cultures were not lost, but they were changed by this process, even as the expatriate Macedonians and Greeks found their own culture changed as they adapted to their new environments, adopted new customs, and encountered new ideas. In Judea, such "hellenization" showed up in the increased attention to learning the Greek language among elite Judeans, so as to communicate with the dominant class and to present themselves as worthy, educated partners in politics and business; the adoption of Greek names and forms of dress, to present themselves as having more in common with the conquering class than the conquered indigenous peoples; and increasing awareness of Greek cultural knowledge and practice.

There was no necessary correlation between these processes and abandoning the Jewish way of life (that is, continuing to observe Torah), though the elites who most wanted to associate with powerful Gentiles and gain influence and wealth through such associations faced a truly slippery slope in this regard. For example, the family members of a Jew named Tobiah rose to great prominence in Judea through the offices they were granted by Ptolemy III Euergetes, but along the way they clearly winked at some practices that Torah forbade. For example, in a letter to a Gentile associate, Tobiah writes "thanks be to the gods" and includes details about both circumcised and uncircumcised boys being sent as slaves to this associate. Torah forbids any such acknowledgment of other gods, even as a formality, as well as giving a Jew as a slave to a Gentile and leaving slaves uncircumcised. Nevertheless, being willing to be seen by the Greek overlords as "one of our own" potentially brought great advantages.

The Hellenizing "Reform"

After Antiochus III's death, Seleucus IV Philopator (187–175 BCE) came to the throne. He is chiefly remembered for ongoing attempts to raise money to replenish the Seleucid coffers and to pay the installments on the fines imposed by his Roman "allies," including an attempt to seize some of the funds safeguarded in the Temple treasury (Dan 11:20; 2 Macc 3:4-40). This episode highlights not only the audacity of the Seleucid kings and the vulnerability of the Temple but also the internal divisions within the Judean elite, for it is a Jewish faction that informed Seleucus IV about private funds in the Temple treasury in the first place, information offered in the hope of that faction's advancement at the cost of the high priest, Onias III, and his supporters. The failure of Seleucus IV's deputy, Heliodorus, to confiscate this money was regarded as nothing short of a miracle. After Heliodorus returned to Syria, however, he assassinated his king, paving the way for Seleucus IV's brother, Antiochus IV Epiphanes (175–164 BCE), to seize power in place of his nephews (1 Macc 1:10; Dan 7:8, 20; 11:21).

At this point, the more progressive party among the Judean elite made a bold move. Jeshua, who took the name Jason, was the high priest's younger brother. He disagreed with Onias's more conservative policies and, supported by a large faction (remembered as "renegades" in 1 Macc 1:11), offered a substantial bribe to Antiochus to be appointed high priest in Onias's place. Jason promised 150 talents more for permission to refound Jerusalem as a Greek city organized according to a Greek constitution. Antiochus welcomed both the additional revenues and the prospect of a more fully integrated Judea, both of which would be congenial to his own plans to try to conquer Egypt. Onias was removed from office (Dan 11:22), and would eventually succumb to foul play (2 Macc 4:32-34).

Jason and his party drew up a list of citizens for the new Jerusalem, no doubt including primarily those Jewish elites sympathetic to the new hellenizing agenda. A senate was also formed from this pool. A gymnasium—the basic educational institution in Greek cities—was built in the shadow of the Temple, where Jerusalem's elite youths would be formally trained in Greek language, literature, learning, and athletics. The Torah no longer functioned as the basis for civil and political law, though it still regulated private religious life and the Temple practice (1 Macc 1:10-15; 2 Macc 3–4). Perhaps because the Jews' religious life was not impinged upon, there appears to have been no open resistance to the political transformation of the city. It is important to recognize that the initiative for more radical hellenization came from the Judean elites themselves (Dan 11:30; 1 Macc 1:11-15; 2 Macc 4:7-15), and not as a result of an alleged program of unifying the kingdom with a single cult and culture on Antiochus's part (against 1 Macc 1:41-43).

The situation began to deteriorate when, in 172 BC, part of the progressive faction shifted its allegiance to a certain Menelaus, who was made high priest in Jason's stead after promising Antiochus IV three hundred talents more than even Jason was paying annually. The overt buying and selling of the most sacred office became increasingly problematic for the Judeans, all the more as Menelaus was not even a member of a high priestly family (as were Jason and Onias). Jason fled Jerusalem, but retained a large number of supporters among the elite. Menelaus was unable to pay Antiochus the promised sums, and so turned to raiding the Temple treasury himself to make at least partial payments (2 Macc 4:27-32). This ongoing practice resulted in the death of Lysimachus, Menelaus's brother and deputy, in a riot (2 Macc 4:39-42). Members of the senate finally brought formal complaints against Menelaus before Antiochus, but Menelaus was able to bribe his way out of trouble (even having his accusers executed; 2 Macc 2:43-47).

In 169 BCE, Ptolemy VI Philometor (181–146 BCE) instigated a war with Antiochus IV by invading Palestine, but was soundly defeated. Antiochus planned to use this as an occasion to take Egypt himself, but he failed in his attempt. Returning from Egypt, he stopped in Jerusalem to raid the Temple treasury for the value of the metal content of its sacred vessels of gold and silver. Antiochus no doubt considered this his due, as Menelaus was ever behind in tribute, but this served only to increase the already volatile anti-Seleucid sentiments. The following year, Antiochus IV invaded Egypt a second time (Polybius, *Histories* 28.18–23). He would have succeeded, had not Ptolemy VI appealed to Rome—the "ally" of the Ptolemies as well as the

Seleucids—for help. Ships from "Kittim" (Dan 11:30) arrived in Alexandria carrying a Roman legate who ordered Antiochus to abandon his efforts to take Egypt at the risk of instigating war with Rome. Antiochus, of course, complied, and set out for his own territory, defeated by Rome's command after winning by force of arms.

During this campaign, a rumor spread that Antiochus had been killed in battle. Jason seized this opportunity to return to Jerusalem at the head of a sizable army (raised, perhaps, with Ptolemy's support) to regain control, besieging Menelaus and his supporters in the citadel. Antiochus received word of this attack and, regarding it as a revolt against his own rule, responded by brutally slaughtering thousands in Jerusalem before liberating Menelaus (Dan 11:30-31). By the time Antiochus arrived, Jason had already withdrawn from Jerusalem, suggesting that the tumult in Jerusalem gave Jewish resistance its first opportunity to emerge, both driving out Jason and continuing the siege against Menelaus (thus Tcherikover 1959, 186–88). Menelaus once again led Antiochus into the Temple treasury to pay the latter his due tribute.

The flames of resistance, however, had now been kindled. In early 167, Antiochus had to send troops under the command of Apollonius to pacify Jerusalem yet again (2 Macc 5:23b-26; 1 Macc 1:29-32). Apollonius established a fortified area that would be called the "Akra," housing both a foreign military garrison and, in times of duress, the hellenized citizens of Antioch-at-Jerusalem (1 Macc 1:33-36).

Many Jews fled Jerusalem for the countryside. Many lost their homes and were relocated in order to furnish the settled soldiers with housing. The most dramatic consequence concerned the worship in the Temple, which now had to serve as the holy place for all citizens of "Antioch-at-Jerusalem," whether Greek, Syrian, or Judean. The sacred space was redecorated and furnished accordingly, and its ceremonies changed or expanded to accommodate the practices of the settled soldiers. This change in cult practice would be remembered in the sources as the "disgusting and destructive thing," or, in more traditional language, the "abomination of desolation" (1 Macc 1:54; see also Dan 11:31; 12:11). The precise nature of the worship "reforms" remains a mystery. Was the "desolating monstrosity" (Dan 11:31) a newly introduced idol, as one would expect for non-Jewish worship? Was it simply a matter of creating a new, inclusive cult or making room for multiple cults? What is clear is that faithful Jews could no longer bring themselves to worship in the Temple, which even many Jews who were avid promoters of Hellenism now regarded as desecrated.

Resistance only increased in the face of these developments, with the result that Antiochus authorized the repression of the practice of Judaism in Judea altogether. If Judean resistance was rallied around "zeal for the Torah," then the practice of Torah itself stood in the way of procuring the peace of Jerusalem and would have to be eliminated. Practices most symbolic of Jewish exclusivism were particularly targeted. Circumcising one's infant son brought the death penalty, as did possession of a copy of the scroll of the Law. Symbolic acts of acquiescence to, and acceptance of, the religious pluralism of the new Antioch-at-Jerusalem were sought out, and authorities latched onto the idea of having Jews eat a morsel of pork (1 Macc 1:44-50, 57-63; 2 Macc 6:1, 8-11, 18–7:42). This persecution claimed many victims, whose devotion to Torah even to the point of death fanned the fire of zeal for the Law and the flames of resistance into a conflagration the likes of which Antiochus and Menelaus had never anticipated.

The Maccabean Revolt

While there are some conflicting data in the two principal sources (1 and 2 Maccabees), a generally reliable picture of the course of the revolution still emerges. During the Hellenizing Crisis, a priest named Mattathias left Jerusalem, together with his sons (John, Simon, Judas, Eleazar, and Jonathan), for the village of Modein, where he raised up a guerrilla army (1 Macc 2:1-28). At first, they attacked not Gentiles, but Jews who had left behind the Torah-observant way of life. They sought, in effect, to reverse the trend of disobedience in Judea, going so far as to forcibly circumcise boys who had been left uncircumcised by their fearful or compromising parents (1 Macc 2:44-48; 3:5-8), and so to restore God's favor toward the nation by removing offense.

After Mattathias died, his most able son, Judas, led the revolution. Under him, the movement gained momentum and began to attack the soldiers of the occupying force. The Seleucid officials did not invest sufficient military resources into squelching the rebellion. Judas and his freedom fighters thereby won some early victories, which caused both their numbers to swell and the Seleucid soldiers to lose morale. In 165 and 164 BCE, the Seleucid government began to dispatch larger forces, but the number of rebels kept pace and Judas continued to prevail. This led to a temporary cease-fire, and Lysias, the Seleucid general in charge of operations, withdrew (1 Macc 3:10–4:35; 2 Macc 8:5-36, with significant differences).

Judas took this opportunity to retake the Temple from Menelaus and the Seleucid garrison at his disposal (1 Macc 4:36-61; 2 Macc 10:1-8). Under Judas's protection, faithful priests removed the pagan paraphernalia and rededicated the altar and Temple to the proper service of the One God. During this hiatus in the larger war, Judas also struck out at Gentile cities in surrounding territories that had been harassing their Jewish residents, bringing the latter back to Judea (1 Macc 5–6; 2 Macc 12:1-9), and continued to fight against any Seleucid forces left in the region (2 Macc 12:10-45). The "desolating monstrosity" came to an end, and the victory was to be commemorated annually in the Festival of Hanukkah. It was at about this time that Antiochus IV died of a mysterious illness, shortly after an unsuccessful attempt to raid the treasury of the sanctuary of Artemis at Elymaïs (in the same city where his father had died plundering the temple of Bel; 1 Macc 6:1-16).

The reprieve, however, was short-lived. Lysias returned with his armies in force (1 Macc 6:18-63; 2 Macc 11:1-15; 13:1-26), prompted in part, no doubt, by the continued unrest in Judea. Intrigues within the Seleucid government back home in Syria, however, prevented him from pressing the war. He urged the young son of Antiochus IV, Antiochus V Eupator, to revoke the decrees against Judaism and to restore their liberty to follow the Torah and to practice their cult in the traditional manner (1 Macc 6:55-63; 2 Macc 11:22-26). Lysias had Menelaus executed as "the cause of all the evils" (2 Macc 13:4). With these concessions granted, many Jews were willing to stop fighting against Seleucid rule. For Judas, his brothers, and their army, however, the war for religious liberty had become a war for political independence, the latter being seen as the only safeguard of the former.

The brother of Antiochus IV, Demetrius I Soter (161–150 BCE), overpowered Antiochus V and his guardian, Lysias (1 Macc 7:1-4; 2 Macc 14:1-2) and turned his attention to securing rebellious Judea. Judas enjoyed one last victory over the first force sent by Demetrius, led by Nicanor (1 Macc 7:26-50; 2 Macc 14:11–15:37), but Judas himself died in battle against an army led by Bacchides, who overran the country and sent the freedom fighters into hiding (1 Macc 9:5-27). The revolution found an able leader, however, in Judas's younger brother, Jonathan, who went on to defeat Bacchides twice, with the result that Demetrius offered terms of peace (1 Macc 9:43-73).

Further internal strife between pretenders to the throne eroded the power of the Seleucid rulers and put Jonathan in an excellent position to negotiate. Demetrius I and his rival, Alexander Balas I (152–145 BCE), vied for Jonathan's military support as the de facto leader of Judea. In addition to many other concessions, Alexander appointed Jonathan to the high priestly office in 153 BCE (1 Macc 10:15-21), and Alexander's successors continued to confirm him as such (1 Macc 10:48–12:38). When Jonathan fell victim to the treachery of another Seleucid pretender named Trypho (1 Macc 12:39-53; 13:12-30), the people chose his last surviving brother, Simon, to lead them (1 Macc 13:1-9).

Simon was confirmed in the office of high priest in his brother's stead, and the office would remain in the Hasmonean family until 37 BCE, when Herod the Great would hand the last Hasmonean ruler over to the Romans for execution and receive, for his part in suppressing a rebellion, authority over Judea as Rome's client king. Simon fought on behalf of Demetrius II against Trypho, and was rewarded for his loyalty by being allowed to remove the Seleucid troops stationed in the Akra in Jerusalem. This was a very important symbolic representation of the removal, at last, of the "yoke of the Gentiles" in 142 BCE, marking a new era of Judea as an independent state after four hundred years of foreign domination (1 Macc 13:41-52).

The Rise and Fall of the Hasmonean Dynasty

After Simon was murdered along with two of his sons by the governor of Jericho, Simon's surviving son, John Hyrcanus I (135–104 BCE), became leader and high priest. After some initial difficulties with the Seleucid king Antiochus VII Sidetes (139–129 BCE), John Hyrcanus was able to expand his borders north past Samaria (which he destroyed, along with the Samaritan temple at Gerizim), south into Idumea, forcing the inhabitants of the latter region to accept circumcision and adopt the Jewish way of life, and east into the Transjordan (Josephus, *Ant.* 13.9.1 §§254–258; 13.10.2-3 §§275–283). Hyrcanus had intended for his wife to become queen in his place, but his eldest son, Judah Aristobulus I (104–103 BCE), intended to enjoy both the high priesthood and civil rule. He killed his mother and imprisoned three of his brothers, eventually executing one of them (Josephus, *Ant.* 13.11.1-2 §§301–313). Aristobulus adopted the title "king" in addition to "high priest" (Josephus, *Ant.* 13.301). He expanded his domain into upper Galilee and Iturea, requiring the inhabitants of the latter to convert to Judaism.

After Aristobulus died, his widow, Salome Alexandra, released his remaining two brothers. She married the elder, Alexander Jannaeus (103–76 BCE), making him king and high priest (Josephus, *Ant.* 13.320). Alexander continued to expand the borders of Israel, retaking control over the coastland from Gaza to Dora as well as the Decapolis (Josephus, *Ant.* 13.15.4 §§395–397). However, Alexander also roused significant internal opposition and responded brutally to the same. So intolerable was his rule that a number of Jews appealed for help to the Seleucid king Demetrius III. Although Demetrius defeated Alexander in battle at Shechem and imposed terms on their behalf, after his withdrawal Alexander exacted a cruel vengeance from his opponents, crucifying eight hundred Jews and butchering their wives and children before their eyes (Josephus, *Ant.* 13.14.2 §380).

After his death, Salome Alexandra (76–67 BCE) rose to the civil power, while their elder son, John Hyrcanus II, functioned as high priest and was to become king upon his mother's death. The younger brother, Judah Aristobulus II (67–63 BCE), coveted both titles for himself (see Josephus, *Ant.* 14.1.1–14.4.5 §§1–79; *J. W.* 1.6.1–1.7.7 §§120–158). As his mother lay dying, Aristobulus mobilized his supporters to seize twenty strongholds throughout Judea, appropriated the money stashed in these fortresses to hire a mercenary army, and declared himself high priest and king. At the instigation of an Idumean named Antipater (the father of Herod), Hyrcanus fled to King Aretas of Petra for support, returning with an army to seize back his birthright.

At this point, Rome decisively intervened in Judean affairs. Pompey the Great ordered Hyrcanus to lift the siege of Jerusalem and summoned both brothers to present their cases. A third party of citizens appears to have presented its own case against the tyranny and brutality of Hasmonean rule. Pompey instructed both brothers to keep the peace until he rendered a decision. Aristobulus and his supporters, however, were not confident in their case, and fortified Jerusalem against Pompey. The supporters of Hyrcanus opened the city gates to Pompey, whose army besieged Aristobulus's supporters in the Temple, eventually gaining entry and slaughtering many. Pompey and his officers went into the holy places, an act of desecration that made a strong impact on contemporary Jews. Pompey appointed Hyrcanus high priest, but gave political authority to a senate. The regions that Hyrcanus's uncle and grandfather had conquered were restored to independence (under Rome), and Judea itself became a Roman province and was required to pay an annual tribute. The dynasty of those who had brought freedom and independence to Judea had crumbled under the weight of oppressive policies and internal strife, leaving Judea once again under the yoke of the Gentiles after a mere eighty years.

Jews in the Diaspora

The above history reflects the events narrated in, and provides the backdrop for, the texts from the Apocrypha written in Judea or its neighboring regions, including Sirach (written in Jerusalem itself prior to the Hellenizing Crisis), Judith, the first half of Baruch, some of the additions to Daniel and Esther, possibly Tobit, and, of course, 1 and 2 Maccabees. Other books in the Apocrypha, like Wisdom of Solomon, 3 and 4 Maccabees, and others of the Additions to Esther, reflect the circumstances and challenges of Jews living outside of their ancestral land in "Gentile" territory. Since the majority of Jews, in fact, lived in "Diaspora" during this period (and forever after), we should give some attention to the various major Jewish communities and how they arose.

Diaspora is a Greek word meaning "scattering," a word frequently applied to the dispersal of the Jewish people. The origins of this scattering are to be found in the Assyrian conquest of the northern tribes of Israel (721 BCE) and the Babylonian conquest of Judah (597 and 587 BCE), which led to the deportation of many Jews from their lands to the lands of their conquerors. When presented with opportunities to return en masse to Judah (in both 538 and 520 BCE; see 2 Chr 36:22-23; Ezra 1:1-4), many Jews chose to stay in Babylon, where they and their parents had built lives and planted roots. Babylon would have a thriving Jewish community for a millennium to come, one that would have greater long-term influence on Judaism than the community in Jerusalem.

Egypt became home to a large Jewish community. Egypt was a place of asylum for people from Judah fleeing the onslaught of Nebuchadnezzar's armies (see Jer 43:1-13). Jews formed a large portion of a military colony in Elephantine established in the sixth or fifth century BCE to help protect Egypt's south border. Tens of thousands of Jews were brought back to Egypt as slaves by Ptolemy I following his seizure of Judea from another general (Antigonus) following Alexander's death, though his son, Ptolemy II, freed the majority (*Let. Aris.* 12-14). The Egyptian Jewish community continued to grow through voluntary migration during the Hellenistic period (as it did in many places, facilitated by the widespread adoption of Greek and the greater ease and safety of travel following Alexander's and his successors' actions). It was a "land of opportunity," given its Greek pharaohs' commitment to developing the area's potential resources. The Hellenizing Crisis and the Maccabean Revolt also fueled fresh migrations to Egypt. It was during this period that Onias IV, son of the murdered high priest Onias III, came to

Leontopolis with his party, building a temple there where he could exercise his priestly birthright. Most of Egypt's Jews lived in the seaport of Alexandria, chiefly in two of the city's five districts, though Gentiles lived among them and Jews lived throughout the other districts as well. Alexandria had the largest Jewish population outside of Palestine.

Strategic military resettlement on the part of Hellenistic rulers—moving nonindigenous soldiers into a recently acquired territory—accounts for the beginnings (or, at least, significant expansions) of several Jewish communities. Ptolemy I sent a large number of Jews to Cyrene for this purpose, and Antiochus III resettled two thousand Jewish families from Mesopotamia in his new frontier of Lydia and Phrygia, providing them with land and allowing them to continue to live by their ancestral laws (Josephus, *Ant.* 12.3.4 §§148–153). Ongoing voluntary migration continued to swell Jewish communities in cities throughout those regions and beyond.

Syrian Antioch, in close proximity to Judea, was a draw as early as the third century BCE. Less is known about the beginnings of Jewish communities in Greece, but many were well established by the early Roman imperial period. The origins of the important Jewish community in Rome are also unknown, but this presence is established by the second century BCE. Where Roman historians discuss the Jewish population of Rome, it is, regrettably, almost always in connection with a (temporary) expulsion of Jews from the capital, most often related to the conversion of high-ranking Romans or their wives to this foreign, Eastern superstition. While the largest populations of expatriate Jews were to be found in a few major Diaspora centers like Alexandria, Syrian Antioch, Babylon, and Rome, Jewish communities could be found in cities throughout the Mediterranean. In the words of Strabo the Greek geographer, "They have reached every town, and it is hard to find a place in the world whither this race has not penetrated and where it has not obtained a hold" (quoted in Josephus, *Ant.* 14.7.2 §115).

Jews living in Diaspora in the Mediterranean had to become fluent in Greek, the "common" language of the various peoples, and, to some extent, the indigenous language of their neighbors. The degree to which large numbers of Diaspora Jews adopted the Greek language to the neglect and eventual loss of Hebrew and Aramaic is seen most dramatically in translations of the Jewish Scriptures into Greek (conveniently referred to as "the" Septuagint) as early as the mid-third century BCE. This brought the Jewish Scriptures more directly into conversation with the philosophies and ethics of the Greek world, representing key scriptural ideals with words that now resonated with

Greek conversations about piety and virtue. Jews in Antioch or Alexandria could also display a very high degree of acculturation in terms of adopting Greek dress, forms of entertainment, and social and aesthetic customs. They could also display significant familiarity with Greek literature, drama, and other areas of cultural knowledge.

Once again, knowledge and appropriation of Greek culture did not automatically correlate with being less devoted to the distinctively Jewish way of life laid down in the Torah, as the author of 4 Maccabees or Philo of Alexandria would demonstrate. Some Jews, however, did abandon their distinctive way of life in favor of better access to networking, acceptance, and advancement in the Greco-Roman world. An uncommon but dramatic example is Philo's nephew, Tiberius Julius Alexander, who apostatized from Judaism and eventually went on to become procurator of Judea (46–48 CE) and prefect of Egypt (68–? CE), doing his fellow Jews no favors.

Though making their home, often for generations, in foreign lands, Diaspora Jews remained connected with their ancestral homeland in a number of very practical ways. Jewish males in Judea and abroad paid a self-imposed half-shekel tax in support of the Temple sacrifices, often sending tithes to the Temple as well. They appear to have viewed this as a privilege to be jealously guarded, and not a burden. Jews with the means would also travel to Jerusalem on religious pilgrimage, especially for the Festivals of Passover, Pentecost, and Booths. While this was probably a rare event in the lives of most Jews, it nevertheless established deep feelings of connection with the ancestral land and enhanced their common bond and sense of belonging, as they worshiped together with Jews from Judea and every land (Philo, *Spec.* 1.69–70; Josephus, *Ant.* 4.8.7 §§203–204).

This connection expressed itself in many other ways as well, both formal and informal. Jews in Jerusalem sent 2 Maccabees to their fellow Jews in Egypt, prefixing two letters (2 Macc 1:1–2:18) asking them to observe the newly established Festival of Hanukkah (a festival that, in turn, would affirm their connection with the fortunes of the homeland). The grandson of the Jerusalem wisdom teacher Ben Sira brought a copy of his grandfather's collected instructions to Egypt and translated it there for the edification of the Jewish community. Jews in Rome turned out en masse to show support for a delegation from Jerusalem to the emperor Augustus. Jews in Syria used nonviolent resistance to deter the governor from obeying the emperor Caligula's command to install in the Jerusalem Temple the statue of himself that he had sent. This connection with their ancestral land and people also enhanced

33

Diaspora Jews' sense of identity and sense of distinctiveness from the people around whom they spent most of their lives.

Jews had several different perspectives on the fact of Diaspora. Many Judean Jewish authors filtered the scattering of their people largely through the lens of their biblical history, in which scattering was an element of the whole people's experience of the curses of the covenant, the reward for collective failure to abide by Torah (see, e.g., Bar 2:13-14, 29; 3:8, 10; Tob 14:4b). Historically speaking, this was true: Diaspora was initiated as a consequence of Gentile conquests. Thus, we often find Judean Jews praying that God would "gather" the tribes from the four winds, restoring them to their homeland (Bar 4:36-37; 5:5-6; Sir 36:13, 16; Tob 13:5; 14:5; 2 Esd 13:39-48). Josephus, by contrast, speaks of Diaspora not as the experience of curse, but as God's fulfillment of God's promises to Abraham that his descendants would be more numerous than the stars in the sky, with the result that no one land could hold them (*Ant.* 4.6.4 §§114–116).

Philo, who lived his whole life in Alexandria, regards the Diaspora as the result of the Jewish nation's successful colonization of the inhabited world (a stunning counterpoint to his own people's experience of five centuries of being colonized; *Leg.* 281–282). While Israel remained a kind of spiritual homeland for all Jews, and Jerusalem the "mother city" of all Jews, most Jews in Diaspora continued to regard their immediate location as their "native land" and gave little indication of longing to "return" to Israel (though some do appear to have relocated to Jerusalem; see Acts 6:9, for example).

The synagogue was an essential institution for Diaspora Jews, though it was also important for Jews in Judea and its surrounding regions. Wherever there was a sizable Jewish community, one could find one or more synagogues to support its religious and community life. The Jewish community gathered in the synagogue on the Sabbath for study of the Torah, prayer, and worship. They also gathered there to celebrate the annual Jewish festivals. Internal disputes within the community were resolved there, records maintained and archived there, and the Temple tax safeguarded there. Larger Jewish communities in the Diaspora appear to have been allowed some measure of self-governance, always ultimately answerable to the Gentile authorities. While individual Jews might have become citizens of the city in which they lived, this was hardly a right extended to all members of the Jewish community, the majority of whom were more akin to resident aliens with right of abode.

Texts emanating from the Jewish Diaspora, like Wisdom of Solomon, 3 and 4 Maccabees, and the final form of Greek Esther, will take us deeper into the challenges and concerns of these communities. In particular, these texts display the challenges of living as a faithful Jew when doing so increases the likelihood of alienation from, and rejection by, the people among whom one must live out one's day-to-day existence.

Chapter 3

God, the Law,
and the Covenant

The starting point for theology, ethics, and piety throughout the writings of the intertestamental period (and especially the books of the Apocrypha) is the Torah, the instruction that God gave to Israel through Moses in the Law. Torah was "instruction" insofar as it taught, through examples and through direct legislation, the way to live wisely and advantageously before the God of Israel. Torah was also "law" insofar as it precisely detailed the obligations laid upon the people who had been taken into a covenant relationship with the God of Israel, the fulfillment of which was a necessary part of maintaining that covenant relationship and the benefits it brought to the people of Israel. The books collected in the Apocrypha provide testimony to the value of the Torah for the pious Jew as divine instruction, as guide to maintaining the privileged relationship God initiated with Israel, and as the basis for hope for oneself and the nation in this life and beyond this life and this age. They provide an important counterpoint, in this way, to several voices in the New Testament for whom Christ and Christ's teachings have displaced Torah as the focal point for instruction, identity, and eschatological hope.

The Torah in the Apocrypha

In order to understand the theology of Torah within Second Temple period Judaism, one must shed the false dichotomy between "law" and "grace" at the outset. While this became a vitally important contrast for Paul as he sought to understand the significance of the death of Jesus and the giving of the Holy Spirit to both Jews and Gentiles as a consequence of this act of

37

beneficence, it was not a meaningful contrast for the authors of the apocryphal books. The giving of the Torah itself was a supreme act of "grace"—of generosity and unmerited privilege—on God's part toward Israel.

This emerges nowhere more clearly than in Sirach. In keeping with the personification of "Wisdom," the consort after whom every sage seeks, in Proverbs 8, Ben Sira depicts this figure of Wisdom telling her story:

> "I came forth from the mouth of the Most High,
>   and I covered the earth like a mist.
> I lived in the heights,
>   and my throne was in a pillar of cloud.
> I alone encircled the vault of heaven
>   and walked in the depths of abysses." (Sir 24:3-5)

Wisdom is a universal figure, active "among every people and nation" (Sir 24:6), but God makes Wisdom to become God's special gift to one particular people:

> "I sought a resting place among all of these.
>   In whose allotted territory should I make my home?
>
> "Then the creator of all things gave me a command;
>   the one who created me pitched my tent
>   and said, 'Make your dwelling in Jacob,
>   and let Israel receive your inheritance.' . . .
>   and so I was established in Zion. . . .
> He made the dearly loved city my resting place
>   and established my authority in Jerusalem.
> I took root in a glorified people;
>   among the people the Lord chose for his inheritance." (Sir 24:7-8, 10-12)

The Jewish sages, including Ben Sira himself, had always looked abroad for wisdom as well as to the local tradition of Israel. Ben Sira, however, is the first to assert that God's special relationship with Israel—God's "election" of Israel to be God's own people—means that God has also given Israel the special grace of planting Wisdom herself at the heart of their formation as a people. Where is she to be found, then? "All these things are in the covenant scroll of the Most High God, the Law that Moses commanded us, the inheritance of the congregations of Jacob" (Sir 24:23). The Torah represents God's special provision for the people of Israel, giving them immediate access to

Wisdom and all her benefits, such that Ben Sira can claim, "If you want to find Wisdom, then keep the commandments, and the Lord will supply her to you in vast quantities," and that "all wisdom involves doing the Law" (Sir 1:26; 19:20).

The author of Baruch gives voice to the same convictions. Wisdom was not to be found "in Canaan or seen in Teman," nor among "Hagar's children, who seek earthly understanding" (Bar 3:22-23); that is to say, it was not to be found in the nations surrounding Israel. The great giants of old, mighty warriors though they were, were not graced with Wisdom by God (Bar 3:26-27). God's domain "is great and has no end; it is high and immeasurable," such that no one could seize Wisdom to bring her down out of the clouds (Bar 3:25, 29). In an act of supreme kindness to a particular people, then, "God found her by his understanding . . . and gave her to his child Jacob, to Israel, whom he loved" (Bar 3:32, 36), choosing this people from among the innumerable peoples within God's vast domain. Wisdom "appeared on the earth and lived among humans," taking on corporeality in the form of "the scroll containing God's commandments, the Law that exists forever" (Bar 3:37; 4:1). The author of Baruch concludes his poem on Wisdom by exclaiming, "Israel, we are blessed because we know what is pleasing to God" (Bar 4:4). The knowledge of the way of life that pleases God is considered a great gift— a sign of being "blessed," privileged above every other nation, shown special favor (grace) by the God of heaven and earth.

The author of 4 Maccabees would also speak of Torah as a sign of God's gracious provision for human beings to live fully in line with their design, as it were, as rational and moral beings:

> When God formed human beings, God planted emotions and character traits inside them. At that time, God also set the mind on the throne in the middle of the senses, to function as a holy governor over them all. God gave the Law to the mind. Whoever lives in line with the Law will rule over a kingdom that is self-controlled, just, good, and courageous. (4 Macc 2:21-23)

In keeping with Greco-Roman ethical philosophy, this author regards human life as a contest between the rational faculty and the "passions" (emotions, cravings, character traits, and the like) for mastery over the individual person. If the passions gain the upper hand, the individual is driven toward a life of vice and moral failure. The passion of fear or experience of pain drives one toward cowardice; greed drives one toward injustice and away from virtuous generosity; cravings for food and for sex, and the prospect of pleasurable sensations, drive one toward immoderation in eating and toward crossing the lines safeguarding the sanctity of marriage. If the rational faculty maintains the upper hand, however, the individual will be able to live in line with socially valued virtues and attain the nobility of character and life appropriate for morally capable beings.

While Greco-Roman moralists also pursued the virtues of justice, courage, self-control, and prudence, the author of 4 Maccabees regards the Torah as God's special gift to human beings (particularly to Israel) to empower and direct the rational faculty so that the pious Jew could indeed attain these virtues through mastery of the passions. He agrees with Ben Sira (e.g., Sir 1:14-18, 26-27; 19:20) that "wisdom" is to be gained strictly through the "instruction provided by the Law, through which we learn about divine matters reverently and human matters to our advantage" (4 Macc 1:17).

The Torah provides the necessary formative discipline for stretching and strengthening the rational faculty for its contests against the passions and drives (see also Sir 6:18-37). The rules about forbidden foods provide occasions to exercise the virtue of self-control, preparing one for greater contests (1:31-35). The commandments regulating lending money and releasing debts, or forbidding a farmer from going through his or her field a second time (to ensure that something would be left from the harvest for the poor who would glean the field), trained a person to overcome greed and learn to be generous (2:8-9). The rules for engagement against an enemy guarded against the excesses of wrath, forcing self-restraint (2:14). The giving of the Torah was therefore a show of great sympathy and generosity on the part of the Creator, who thus provided the means by which his creatures could attain their full potential as moral beings.

The authors of the Apocrypha thus articulate a theology of grace and election in which the giving and the doing of the Torah play an integral part. Following the Torah is not understood to be a matter of earning God's favor, but of responding well to the favor God has already shown in the giving of the Law in the first place. A second striking feature of the view of the Law in these texts is the conviction that living by the Law is very much within human reach, and not an exercise in futility.

Ben Sira reads the second creation account in Genesis 2–3 as evidence that, when God "created humanity at the beginning, . . . he left them to the power of their choices" (Sir 15:14). Human beings are free and empowered to do what is good or what is evil. Even if humanity first exercised their will or inclination (in Hebrew, their *yetzer*) in the direction of disobedience, each new human being has the same choice and the same freedom: "If you choose to, you will keep the commandments, and keep faith out of goodwill" (15:15).

Ben Sira has in mind Moses' words near the close of Deuteronomy, in which human capacity to follow the Torah and enjoy its blessings is strictly and unambiguously affirmed:

> Look here! Today I've set before you life and what's good versus death and what's wrong. If you obey the LORD your God's commandments that I'm commanding you right now by loving the LORD your God, by walking in his ways, and by keeping his commandments, his regulations, and his case laws, then you will live and thrive, and the LORD your God will bless you in the land you are entering to possess. . . . I have set life and death, blessing and curse before you. Now choose life—so that you and your descendants will live. (Deut 30:15-16, 19)

Ben Sira echoes this scriptural text in his own teaching:

> He has put fire and water before you;
>   you can stretch out your hand for whichever you choose.
> Life and death are in front of human beings;
>   and they will be granted whichever they please. (Sir 15:16-17)

While in many ways he affirms God's providential ordering of creation, he denies that this extends to the life choices individual persons will make, removing God's sovereignty as an excuse for sin (15:11-13). Most important, at no point does he speak of Torah as an impossible ideal, such that human failure is "built into" the system. The power to obey Torah is, indeed, within human grasp.

The author of 4 Maccabees, writing at least two centuries later, maintains the same positive view of Torah and human ability to do what Torah commands. In a passage that offers a striking contrast to Paul's commentary on the commandment "You shall not covet," this Jewish orator declares that the fact that "the Law says, 'You will not desire your neighbor's wife or anything that belongs to your neighbor,'" offers decisive proof that "clear thinking is able to control desires" (4 Macc 2:5-6). The author believes that God would never have commanded that which is impossible. The presence of the command, therefore, implies the possibility of doing what is commanded, and, hence, the power of the devout mind to master sinful desires and to choose obedience and virtue instead. Paul, a near-contemporary, does not speak for all Jews when he claims that the commandment actually gives "sin" the opportunity to emerge and gain the mastery over the individual:

> I wouldn't have known sin except through the Law. I wouldn't have known the desire for what others have if the Law had not said, *Don't desire what others have.* But sin seized the opportunity and used this commandment to produce all kinds of desires in me. . . . So the commandment that was intended to give life brought death. (Rom 7:7-8, 10)

This is not to say that Jews besides Paul did not struggle with the difficulty of keeping the covenant and overcoming the power of the sinful inclination, the *yetzer ha-ra*. The author of the Jewish apocalypse 4 Ezra (2 Esd 4–14) is painfully aware of the forces at work within the human being urging the person to choose against the commandment. Indeed, he regards the bent toward sinning to be all but endemic to human nature as a result of the first person's sin:

> You gave [Adam] one command, and he disobeyed it, and so you immediately appointed death for him and for his descendants. . . . Your glory passed through the four gates of fire, earthquake, wind, and ice so that you would give the Law to Jacob's descendants, the rules to be observed to Israel's offspring.
>
> But you didn't take away from them the inclination to do evil so that your Law might bear fruit in them. The first Adam, burdened with this inclination, disobeyed you and was overcome, but so were all those descended from him. The disease became permanent; the Law was in the people's heart along with the wicked root, and that which was good departed and the wickedness remained. (2 Esd 3:7, 19-22)

Thus, while "Ezra" agrees that the giving of the Torah was an act of God's grace toward one particular nation among all those descended from Adam, he argues that the sinful inclination ends up, in the end, preventing that gift from ever bearing its salvific fruit. Ezra blames God, in effect, for not simply removing the sinful inclination so that the Torah could be easily kept and its covenant blessings readily enjoyed.

In the arguments that follow between Ezra and the archangel Uriel, sent by God to console him and set his thinking straight, Uriel affirms that God is not in any way at fault and that the responsibility for doing what is righteous or sinful in God's sight remains entirely with human beings. The angel declares:

"These are the rules for the contest in which everyone born on earth takes part: Those who are defeated will suffer what you said, but those who conquer will receive what I say. This is the path that Moses declared when he was alive, speaking to the people, *Choose life for yourself . . . so that you may live.*" (2 Esd 7:127-129)

Once again, the foundational text from Deuteronomy 30:19 emerges as a proof that, while obedience may be difficult and require strenuous self-discipline, it is certainly possible. The power of the sinful inclination within the human being does not necessitate—nor excuse—defeat. The image of the "contest," which calls to mind athletic events requiring a great deal of investment and focused effort against difficult adversaries, acknowledges the existential experiences of Jews struggling to follow Torah while also affirming the possibility of overcoming. The prizes for the same more than reward any effort, such that the Jew is called to dedicate himself or herself to practicing the Torah with the same rigor that an athlete gives to training and competing. Moreover, in another manifestation of grace, God labors alongside the dedicated Jew, whom God has "perfected . . . with much effort" (2 Esd 9:22). God may not remove the sinful inclination, but God works alongside the human being to overcome its power, acting as his or her partner in "the contest in which everyone born on earth takes part."

Deuteronomy's Theology of History

Obeying the particulars of the Torah was valued by Jews on a number of counts. First, it was regarded as an appropriate response to the God who had given them the gift of life itself and the gift of knowledge of what pleased God. Honoring the Torah by following its prescriptions was a way that human beings could show their respect for and gratitude toward the God who gave them life in the first place. But Torah also contained the particulars of a covenant that God had made with a particular nation, outlining their responsibilities toward that God and the responsibilities God undertook on their behalf. The reciprocal nature of this agreement was laid out clearly in Deuteronomy, which articulates a theology of history that would impact how the Jewish people made sense of their national fortunes from the decline of the monarchy and exile through the period of domination by the Greek, Hellenistic, and Roman empires. This is perhaps one of the most pervasive topics among the books of the Apocrypha.

Deuteronomy—and thus the larger body of laws, beginning in Exodus, that constitutes Israel's covenant obligations—closes with several chapters outlining the consequences of keeping or failing to keep these covenant obligations. Obeying God "by carefully keeping all his commandments that I am giving you right now" will result in God's exalting Israel "high above all nations on earth" (Deut 28:1). The blessings included within this exaltation concern the fertility of the land and of its inhabitants, the security of the people in urban and rural areas, protection against any enemies who attempt to attack, and honor in the sight of all the neighboring peoples (28:2-14). Disregard for these commandments, however, will bring curses upon the nation: barrenness of land and people, vulnerability to foreign attack and natural plague, and decimation of the population (28:15-46). In particular, God would bring "a distant nation . . . a stern nation that doesn't go easy on the very old or show pity to the very young" to besiege Israel's cities until Israel's inhabitants are taken captive as slaves and scattered "among every nation" (28:49-50, 64).

However, after these curses are inflicted as punishment upon the disobedient nation, if the people "return to the LORD your God, obeying his voice, in line with all that I'm commanding you right now—you and your children—with all your mind and with all your being[, then] the LORD your God will restore you as you were before and will have compassion on you, gathering you up from all the peoples where the LORD your God scattered you" (Deut 30:2-3). God will gather the exiles, restore their homeland, and make the people numerous and prosperous once again. God will help them to keep the covenant, and visit all these curses upon Israel's enemies (30:4-7).

Deuteronomy provides the basic framework within which Jewish writers understood the rise and fall of Israel and Judah, as well as the foundation of hope for restoration: where Jews returned wholeheartedly to the covenant, they could hope for the return of God's favor and their restoration. Many of the writers of the books of the Apocrypha also return to this framework to think about the experience of exile and Diaspora as a result of the Assyrian and Babylonian conquests, to make sense of the ongoing history of the nation's fortunes after the restoration of the Temple (the "Second Commonwealth"), and even to predict the future fortunes of the nation (see, for example, Jdt 5:2-19; 8:18-20). Two texts that particularly engage with Deuteronomy's theology of history are Baruch and 2 Maccabees.

The three major sections of Baruch—its prayer of confession and request for help (1:15–3:8); its poem about returning to Torah, the fount of wisdom (3:9–4:4); and its promise of restoration addressed to Zion in mourning (4:5–5:9)—reinforce the procedure, in effect, for the reversal of national misfortune laid out in Deuteronomy 30. The book opens with a prayer of confession and repentance that Baruch prescribes for the priests and others in Judah to use on behalf of the whole nation. The prayer declares that "justice is on the side of the Lord God," absolving God from any responsibility for the disasters that have overtaken Israel (Bar 1:15-17; 2:6). These are entirely the fault of the people, who neglected their covenant obligations and brought its curses upon their own heads (Bar 1:18-20; 2:1-10). The author brings in several details from Deuteronomy's descriptions of these curses, including the decimation of Israel's numbers (Bar 2:29; Deut 28:62), the pathetic image of mothers consuming their infants because of the desperation of the siege (Bar 2:3; Deut 28:53), and the fulfillment of the threat that God would "bring a distant nation . . . a stern nation that doesn't go easy on the very old or show pity to the very young" (Deut 28:49-50; Bar 4:15).

After owning responsibility, the author of the prayer appeals to God now to turn with mercy toward the people and restore them, since they have come to their senses and again turned in their hearts toward God. Because God has bound himself to Israel as their covenant God, Israel's fortunes reflect on God's power and stature. Therefore, the author incites God now to be reconciled to God's people for the sake of his own reputation: "For your own sake, set us free and give us favor with those who have brought us into exile so that all the earth might know that you are the Lord our God, since Israel and her children carry your name" (Bar 2:14-15; see also Dan 9:19; Pr Azar 22). But hope for deliverance rests primarily on God's promise in Deuteronomy 30:1-5 that God would restore the penitent to their land and those who renewed their obedience to the blessings of the covenant (Bar 2:19-35).

Baruch then addresses the congregation of Israel with a wisdom poem. He explains that they "are in the enemies' land, growing old in a foreign land" (Bar 3:10), because they have not walked in the ways of wisdom, that is, the stipulations of the covenant. This poem focuses the hearer on returning to a wise pattern of living, which is to be found in the distinctive heritage of Israel, specifically in "the scroll containing God's commandments," which is Wisdom on earth (Bar 3:37–4:1). In context, this poem exhorts the readers to pursue the only path available for national recovery—a renewed and wholehearted commitment to living in line with the Torah.

The last segment of Baruch takes on a prophetic coloring, as first "Jerusalem" encourages her exiled children that their condition is the temporary punishment for their sins against the covenant (though Jerusalem also commiserates with just how rigorous this punishment has been; Bar 4:5-29), and then as the prophet's voice addresses Jerusalem with words of encouragement. Her children will indeed be restored to her when God's anger turns again to mercy (4:30–5:9). In line with Deuteronomy's proclamation, Baruch affirms that it is only by turning to Torah that the prayer of 1:15–3:8 will be answered and the restoration promised in 4:5–5:9 enjoyed. Such an understanding of national fortunes and misfortunes helped to preserve the distinctively Jewish way of life and witness to God in the most politically desperate times, since the way of wisdom was to keep Torah, whether in prosperity or adversity, in the land or in exile.

Second Maccabees shows how important Deuteronomy's theology of history remained as a framework for understanding not only Israel's historic crises but also new crises that rocked the nation. Indeed, a particular interest of 2 Maccabees seems to be to give a theological interpretation of the events of the Hellenizing Crisis and Maccabean Revolt (the recent events of 175–161 BCE) in line with this covenant framework.

Unlike 1 Maccabees, this history begins well before the "action" of the Maccabean Revolution and the crisis that precipitated it. The opening scene is one in which "the holy city was living in harmony, and people observed the laws strictly because of Onias the high priest, who was devoted to God and hated evil" (2 Macc 3:1). When the covenant was being duly observed and enforced from above, the nation enjoyed the blessings that God promised in the covenant, to the point that even Gentile rulers subsidized the offerings made at the Temple (2 Macc 3:2). When a renegade Jew convinces the Greco-Syrian king Seleucus IV that he can rightfully confiscate certain funds in the Temple treasury, and Seleucus sends his officer, Heliodorus, to secure the funds, invisible forces prevent Heliodorus from entering the sacred Temple, striking him down (3:3-30). The point of the episode is made explicit later: when the people and their rulers observe the Torah, God protects his Temple and people (5:18), as Deuteronomy promises.

The successors of Onias, however, undermined the place of Torah as the law of the land. First, Jason replaced the Torah with a Greek constitution and its laws for governing the city of Jerusalem, showing a greater zeal for promoting Greek culture than Jewish piety. The author already begins to prepare the readers to interpret the ensuing crisis in light of the Deuteronomic pattern:

For this reason a dangerous situation engulfed them. Those same people to whom they were devoted and whose way of life they wished to imitate became their enemies and inflicted punishment on them. To be ungodly in the face of the divine laws isn't a light matter, as the following events would reveal. (2 Macc 4:16-17)

Becoming "like the nations" must inevitably lead, according to Deuteronomy, to God's using these Gentile powers as a whip in God's hand to chasten Israel for violating the call to remain set apart from the nations for the One God (see Deut 28:49-53).

Then Menelaus, who supplanted Jason, used the Temple treasury as his own purse and led Antiochus IV into the sanctuary himself to allow the latter to collect the tribute due him (when a high priest ought to have defended the holy places from such intrusion). The author again intervenes to comment:

Antiochus was really pleased with himself, not realizing the Lord had become angry for a short time because of the sins of those who lived in the city. For this reason, he had shut his eyes to the holy temple. If they hadn't previously been involved in so many sins, Antiochus would have been forced to abandon his rashness and been defeated at once when he attacked, just like Heliodorus. (2 Macc 5:17-18)

The Heliodorus episode proves that Antiochus's desecration of the holy places was a sign not of God's weakness, but of the truth of Deuteronomy's warnings. Nevertheless, the author also knows that "that which the almighty abandoned in his wrath would again be restored with all glory when the nation was reconciled to the great Lord" (2 Macc 5:20), since the Deuteronomic pattern ended not with Israel's punishment, but rather with its restoration to covenant loyalty and protection.

The suppression of Torah observance, the rededication of the Jerusalem Temple to foreign gods, and the brutal deaths of Jews who continued to circumcise their children, refused to eat forbidden foods, and hid copies of the Torah to preserve them represent the nation's experience of chastisement, the temporary onslaught of the covenant curses. Nevertheless, even as such they were a sign of God's special mercy toward Israel, since they were meant to correct rather than destroy:

These punishments weren't for the destruction of our people but for their discipline. It is a sign of great kindness that those Jews who acted immorally

47

weren't left alone for very long but experienced punishments immediately. With other nations the Lord patiently delays punishment until they fill up the full measure of their sins, but with us he decided to deal differently, and is exacting retribution on us before our sins reach their peak. Therefore, he never withdraws his mercy from us. Although disciplining us with misfortunes, God doesn't forsake his own people. (2 Macc 6:12-16; cf. also 7:16b, 33-35)

At this point, the author turns his attention to a group of martyrs whose loyalty to God and God's covenant to the point of death is the turning point in the story, the offering of obedience that tips the scales again toward Israel's restoration.

God punishes the nation as a collective whole rather than punishing only the guilty individuals within the nation (for example, the radical hellenizers). The martyrs understand their own suffering in the context of the nation's guilt, even though they themselves are, more immediately, suffering precisely because of their *refusal* to break faith with God and God's Law:

We suffer these things because of our own sins against our God. (2 Macc 7:18)

We are suffering because of our own sins. If our living Lord is angry for a short time in order to rebuke and discipline us, he will again be reconciled with his own servants. (2 Macc 7:32-33)

However, because they are also suffering as a result of their own obedience—in contrast to the many in the nation who suffer repression as a result of their disobedience—the martyrs are able to offer themselves voluntarily to God on behalf of their nation, asking God to fill up the measure of the nation's punishment with their own endurance of torture unto death. Speaking to Antiochus IV, who has used every torture imaginable to try to compel these martyrs to eat pork as a symbol of their renunciation of Judaism, the youngest and last-surviving of seven brothers declares:

Just like my brothers, I give up both body and life for the ancestral laws. I call upon God to be merciful to the nation without delay, and to make you confess, after you suffer trials and diseases, that only he is God. Also I hope through me and my brothers to stop the anger of the almighty, who is justly punishing our entire nation. (2 Macc 7:37-38)

As far as the author is concerned, the martyrs' voluntary, obedient deaths are in fact effective for turning away God's wrath. Immediately after this episode, Judas Maccabeus and his army begin to enjoy successes on the field against the Syrian occupation force: "Once he organized his army, the Maccabee couldn't be stopped by the Gentiles, because the Lord's wrath had turned into mercy" (2 Macc 8:5). As the sin of individuals like Jason, Menelaus, and their parties brought punishment upon the nation, so the extraordinary loyalty of individuals can bring about a reversal of the covenant curses.[1]

The following episode in which Judas first defeats a powerful army, led by the Syrian general Nicanor, shows that the favor of the covenant God and the blessings of the covenant had been restored. Once again, "the Jews couldn't be defeated because they followed God's ordained laws" (2 Macc 8:36; cf. 3:39).

Deuteronomy's theology of history forges an inseparable connection between widespread observance of the Torah and the well-being of Israel as a collective whole (national security, as it were). One response to this connection manifested itself in "zeal for the Torah" such as Mattathias, Judas Maccabeus, and their party showed in 1 Maccabees. When a Syrian official comes to the village of Modein and invites Mattathias, a priest and a revered elder there, to sacrifice to a foreign god as a sign of submission to the king's decrees against Jewish exclusivism, Mattathias refuses. When another man from the village steps forward to comply, Mattathias responds by striking down both the official and the apostate with his sword (1 Macc 2:15-25). The author compares Mattathias to Phinehas, who, in his zeal for the Law (2:26, 54), was famous for putting an end to a plague by killing an Israelite male together with his Midianite wife (Num 25:6-15).

Immediately following this episode, Mattathias calls "everyone who is zealous for the Law and supports the covenant" to go with him to the hill country (1 Macc 2:27-28), whence he and his sons stage attacks not only on Gentile soldiers but also on apostate Jews living in the surrounding area: "In their fury, they struck down sinners and renegades. Survivors fled to the Gentiles for safety. . . . They forcibly circumcised boys whom they found uncircumcised within the borders of Israel" (2:44, 46). Judas "hunted and pursued those who broke the Law," and thus "he turned wrath away from Israel" (3:5, 8). Such zeal for the Torah operated by not tolerating transgression in the midst of the people and the land of Israel. It was offered to God as an expression of obedience and radical loyalty to the covenant that, it was hoped, would protect Israel from the consequences of disobedience in its midst. Similar sentiments motivated Paul in his zeal for the Torah to attack

49

Jewish Christians, whose loyalty to the Torah was open to question (Gal 1:13-14; Phil 3:6).

A second response focused on zeal for the Torah did not involve violence *against* others, though it could certainly involve accepting violence perpetrated against oneself. A righteous person might be able to achieve benefits for the nation as a whole by displaying perfect loyalty and obedience to the covenant. This concept shows up in the community at Qumran, where righteous deeds are offered to make atonement for the guilt of the people and for the land (1QS 5:5-6; 8:6). It shows up most clearly, however, in the figures of the martyrs who died prior to the Maccabean Revolt. As already seen, these were righteous individuals who accepted the imposition of torture and death rather than break faith with God's covenant under the pressure of such compulsion. Perhaps the voluntary suffering of the righteous for the sake of the Torah could hasten the reconciliation of God with God's people, whether because the measure of punishment was thus more speedily filled up, or because the righteous could offer their lives as a gift to God on behalf of others in the nation who could then be spared, or because an outstanding display of covenant loyalty could erase the memory, as it were, of a prior display of neglect of the covenant on the part of the nation.

Fourth Maccabees, a Hellenistic Jewish oration based on 2 Maccabees 6–7, shows a considerable development of its source in this regard. The first martyr, the aged priest Eleazar, suffers torture unto death rather than yielding to the tyrant's command to transgress God's Law, and prays:

> God, you know that I could have saved myself; instead, I am being burned and tortured to death for the sake of your Law. Have mercy on your people. Make our punishment sufficient for their sake. Purify them with my blood, and take my life in exchange for theirs. (4 Macc 6:27-29)

Eleazar offers, in effect, a voluntary, costly righteous act as atonement for those who, because of their sins, need "purification." The author comments toward the end of the oration on the collective deaths of the nine martyrs, using further sacrificial language to talk about the significance of the deaths of the righteous: "They exchanged their lives for the nation's sin. Divine providence delivered Israel from its former abuse through the blood of those godly people. Their deaths were a sacrifice that finds mercy from God" (4 Macc 17:21-22). The focus on "blood" and "sacrifice" should not obscure the fact that a Deuteronomistic understanding of events is in view: an exceptional act of covenant loyalty stems the tide of covenant curses and reconciles God to God's people. The combination of sacrificial metaphors and an emphasis on a death voluntarily offered in obedience to God would prove extremely important also to the early Christian movement, which looked to the death of Jesus for the restoration of God's favor toward the circumcised and uncircumcised alike and the expansion of the covenant and its blessings to people of all nations.

The Covenant, God's Justice, and Israel's Hope

The covenant provided the basic framework not only for interpreting the ups and downs of history but also for hope—the individual person's hope for a good life and the nation's hope for survival and prosperity. Several authors of the books of the Apocrypha are concerned to demonstrate how the covenant proves reliable at both levels, and to address the doubts about God and the covenant that inevitably arise when bad things happen to good people and when the wicked prosper.

Ben Sira generally affirmed that observing the commandments of God would lead to the enjoyment of good things in life, whereas neglect of the same would deprive one of good in this life:

> Fear of the Lord will cheer the heart,
>   and it will give gladness, joy, and a long life.
> Things will go well at the end for those who fear the Lord.
>   They will be blessed at the time of death. (Sir 1:12-13)

> If you fear the Lord, you'll lack nothing;
>   if you have it, there's no reason to look for help.
> Fear of the Lord is like an orchard of blessing,
>   and it covers a person more fully than any glory. (Sir 40:26-27)

Ben Sira had to acknowledge, however, the reality that life could be difficult for all people, righteous and renegades alike. He explains this, in part, by appealing to the curse that befell all humankind in the beginning as the result of the sin of the first human being, Adam (Sir 40:1, 11; 41:4, 10; cf. Gen 3:17-19). All are born to endure some degree of difficulty. Nevertheless, Ben Sira tries to affirm that God makes a distinction between the righteous and the unrighteous: "To all flesh, both human and animal, but to sinners seven times more so, come death, blood, strife, sword, catastrophes, famine, ruin, and disease" (Sir 40:8-9). If bad things happen to good people, they happen

51

far more often and with greater severity to the bad. Or, a person's sins catch up with him or her at life's end, inflicting an anxiety and a regret that erase all memory of life's enjoyments (Sir 11: 21, 25-28).

In the face of undeserved suffering, Ben Sira counsels, in the end, endurance supported by the conviction that God's good purposes will work themselves out, and God's wisdom will be revealed, "at its proper time" (Sir 39:17, 34). He also suggests that his disciples confront difficulties and hardships as opportunities for character formation and as tests of their commitment to the discipline of Torah and the godly way of life (2:1-6; 4:15-19; 6:22-31), an orientation toward suffering that will have significant staying power in the centuries to follow (see also Tob 12:13-14; Wis 3:1-9).

There is no room in Ben Sira's thought for reward or punishment beyond death. The righteous will enjoy the blessings of the covenant within their own lives and (or, perhaps only) in the good name and reputation they leave behind them. A person's reputation "will continue after you longer than one thousand great treasures of gold. A good life has a limited number of days, but a good name will continue forever" (Sir 41:12-13). Ben Sira enacts this living memory in his hymn in praise of "famous people" (44:1). The original Hebrew text called these people "people of *ḥesed*," people of covenant loyalty: such people live on, and live well, in the memory of the congregation. By contrast, the bad reputation of the deceased sinner, whose memory is cursed, is a kind of second death.

Ben Sira's musings on the problem of suffering, and especially the problem of Torah-observant persons not actually enjoying the blessings promised in the covenant to the faithful, were not sufficient to meet the demands of the crisis that followed his death. On the eve of the Maccabean Revolt, it was specifically the staunchly Torah-observant who were treated the most shamefully and subjected to torture and execution, with no hope of vindication in this life. Deuteronomy might still explain the collective plight of the nation, but what about God's faithfulness to the individual who was righteous? How could God allow a degrading, painful death—and premature removal from all the blessings of life—to be the ultimate reward of faithfulness?

It was thus during this period that belief in life after death, and particularly divine judgment, rewards, and punishment after death, came to the fore in Jewish theology. Second Maccabees makes an especially important contribution in this regard. In this text, the martyrs and others give prominent expression to the hope of the resurrection of the righteous (2 Macc 7:9, 11,

14, 23, 29; 12:43-45; 14:46), a restoration to life beyond death that specifically involves some kind of embodied existence (2 Macc 7:11; 14:46):

> You . . . may take our present life, but the king of the universe for whose laws we die will resurrect us again to eternal life. (2 Macc 7:9)

> I have received these limbs from heaven, and I give them up for the sake of God's laws. But I hope to recover them from God again. (2 Macc 7:11)

> Death at the hands of humans is preferable, since we look forward to the hope that God gives of being raised by him. But for you there will be no resurrection to life. (2 Macc 7:14)

> The creator of the world—who brought about the beginning of humanity and searched out the origin of all things—will again mercifully give you both spirit and life, since you disregard yourselves because of his laws. (2 Macc 7:23)

> Our brothers, who endured pain for a short time, have been given eternal life under God's covenant, but you will suffer the penalty of your arrogance by the righteous judgment of God. (2 Macc 7:36)

The hope for a resurrected life is rooted in the conviction that the God who created all that is out of nothing can certainly re-create a person beyond death and the destruction of the physical body (2 Macc 7:28; van Henten 1997, 178–80). Belief in the individual's survival beyond death allows the author to continue to affirm God's justice and the absolute value of the covenant: God is faithful to the covenant promises and curses in regard to the nation in this life, and to the individual person as well, whether this justice is served in this life or only beyond death (e.g., when the faithful Jew must suffer alongside the renegade because of God's punishment of the nation).

The author of Wisdom of Solomon also devotes the opening five chapters of his book to the problem of the righteous not receiving the benefits of covenant loyalty in this life—and the equal problem of the ungodly prospering, often at the direct expense of the righteous. He sees the apostates and ungodly flourishing in this life by following the philosophy of "might makes right" (see Wis 2:11), gaining wealth at the expense of the vulnerable, giving no thought to observing the covenant. He sees them target the Torah-observant, testing their claim that God protects the righteous and opposes the ungodly, thinking to disprove these claims by putting the righteous to a shameful death (2:12-20). The ungodly, however, have lost sight of the fact that "God created humans to live forever" and has prepared a reward for holiness (2:22-23). The righteous may not enjoy the promised blessings of long life and abundant descendants, but these blessings pale in comparison with the immortal blessings that attend virtue (Wis 4:1, 3, 7-15; 5:15-16). In the end, the ungodly will stand before God, see the reward of the righteous person whom they have oppressed, and confess their stupidity and the wisdom of the Torah-observant (5:1-13).

Some Jewish authors have given up altogether on expecting to see justice done in "this age," but they do not therefore give up on the covenant or the fundamental principle of Deuteronomy that loyalty to the Torah brings blessing and neglect of the same brings curse. The author of 4 Ezra, for example, regards this world to have been ruined by Adam's sin and its repercussions throughout the human race:

> The world is indeed rushing to its end. Indeed, it can't bring the things that are promised to the just during this age, because this world is full of sadness and sickliness. The evil about which you asked me has been sown, and its full harvest hasn't yet come. If that which was sown isn't reaped, and the place where evil has been sown hasn't departed, the field where good is sown won't come. (2 Esd 4:26-29)

This present age is the time in which the consequences of the sinful actions of all humanity must be suffered, a crop that is far from fully sown, let alone reaped. The righteous will not be able to enjoy the rewards promised for their loyalty in this corrupted world. But God, being just, has made provision: "Because of this the Most High made not one world but two" (2 Esd 7:50). God has prepared the world to come as the venue in which God's just recompense to both the righteous and the ungodly will be realized. Because the author can peer into that world, as it were, through the medium of apocalyptic vision, he is able to reinforce the reliability of the basic framework of Deuteronomy for his readers.

The ideology of Israel's election, the promises of restoration in Deuteronomy, and the firm conviction that God is just and reliable provide hope not only for the reward of the individual but also for the eventual restoration of the nation. The last word of Deuteronomy is not punishment, but restoration: when Israel returns to the Lord and to living in line with God's instruction, God will restore Israel to its land and its glory. In time of prosperity or punishment, the covenant relationship between God and Israel is never broken. Israel remains God's people, possession, and purchase among all the nations (Add Esth C:8-9). God's reputation among the nations remains bound to Israel's fortunes: for God to give up on his people would be, in effect, to admit defeat before the false gods of the other nations (Add Esth C:20-22).

Continuing to live under Gentile domination and dispossessed from their ancestral land, Jewish authors looked forward to the inevitable time of restoration, when God would be reconciled to God's people, end the domination of foreign powers, gather the exiles and scattered Israelites, and restore the kingdom of Israel. This hope should encourage Jews to turn to God even in the midst of exile, and to renew their commitment to live according to the covenant—and thus to spur them on to the very thing that will make the hope a reality:

> Bear witness to him, Israelites,
>> in the presence of the nations,
>> because he has scattered you among them. . . .
> He will punish you for your unjust acts,
>> but he will also show all of you mercy and gather you together
>> out of all the nations among which you have been scattered.
> When you turn to him with all your heart and [all your] being to act
>> sincerely before him,
>> then he will turn to you and never hide his face from you again.
> (Tob 13:3, 5-6)

Renewal of covenant obedience among the people remains the fulcrum point for renewing the experience of God's favor, and hence the restoration of national identity, independence, and security.

Perhaps the most striking example of wrestling with the issues of election and covenant in the Apocrypha is to be found in 2 Esdras 3–14, or "4 Ezra." This author writes in the aftermath of the failed Jewish Revolt against Rome in 66–70 CE, addressing it fictively from the vantage point of the destruction of the First Temple by Babylon. He has witnessed not only Rome's devastation of Judea and Jerusalem—a development that, in itself, is perfectly comprehensible within the framework of Deuteronomy—but also Rome's ongoing prosperity and expansion for decades following its actions against the Holy City and its Temple. Where, he asks, is the justice in that? Judea might have been rightly judged by God for failing to keep the obligations of the covenant, but they still have the distinction of being the only people on the face of the planet to *care* about the God of Abraham and to *try* to keep his Law:

> Are the lives of Babylon's inhabitants any better? Is that why Babylon has gained dominion over Zion? . . . Does Babylon do better than Zion? Has any other nation known you besides Israel? What tribes have believed your covenants as have these tribes of Jacob? . . . I have traveled widely among the nations and seen them enjoying abundance while not giving your commandments a thought. . . . When have those who live on earth not sinned in your sight, or what other nation has observed your commandments as has ours? (2 Esd 3:28, 31-33, 35)

"Ezra" continues to press his case. If God really chose Israel from among all the other nations, why do these other nations continue to exercise domination over Israel (2 Esd 5:23-30)? If God created this world for Israel, why does Israel not enjoy its fruits while those nations that are not worth spit in God's sight devour Israel itself (6:55-59)? How is "election" meaningful given our national fortunes and the difficulty of living up to the rigors of the covenant obligations, so as to attain the covenant promises (3:4-27)?

The angel Uriel provides answers to these questions, affirming the ongoing validity of election, of the covenant, and of the promises of Deuteronomy—but with significant redefinition. First, "election" pertains not to all ethnic Jews, but to "those who stored up faith as a treasure" with God (2 Esd 6:5), who "have struggled hard to overcome the evil thought fashioned within them so that it wouldn't lead them astray from life to death" (7:92). Covenant blessings await *this* Israel after death, but also after God's decisive interventions in the history of this world. The author of 4 Ezra has a well-developed concept of a Messiah figure. As befits a visionary deeply concerned about justice in international affairs, the Messiah's first function is to indict Rome for its rule of terror and violence, its oppression of the weak, its repression of the truth, and its insolence (11:41-43). "Babylon" will finally be overturned, making room for the kingdom of God's Son on Mount Zion and the renewal of Jerusalem in splendor, into which the scattered elect will be gathered from every corner (13:27-50; 10:25-27, 50-59).

This apocalypse ends by directing the readers back to the Torah, which is given afresh through Ezra. After all his questioning, the author is able to affirm the validity of the covenant and its promises as "the path" for all "who want to live in the last days" (2 Esd 14:22):

> Our fathers . . . received the Law of life, but they didn't keep it, and you also transgressed after them. You were given land by allotment in the region of Zion. You and your fathers did evil and didn't keep the ways that the Most

High had commanded you. Since he is a just judge, in time he took away from you what he granted. Now you are here, and your relatives live even farther away. If then you will rule your mind and instruct your heart, you will be kept alive, and after death you will attain mercy. (2 Esd 14:29-34)

Deuteronomy's explanation of history remains a valid one—and, more significantly, its promise of life for those who renew their obedience to the Torah remains valid as well, even in the wake of the utter devastation of Jerusalem in 70 CE.

Chapter 4

The Apocrypha and Jewish Ethics

Even though their status as canonical Scripture has been continuously questioned (see chapter 8), the books of the Apocrypha were always appreciated—even by the Protestant Reformers—for the "example of life and instruction of manners" that they provided.[1] Ethical topics are especially foregrounded in Tobit, Ben Sira, and 4 Maccabees, though other books, like Wisdom of Solomon, make important contributions to promoting a virtuous way of life. These texts also raise some ethical dilemmas, however, such as Judith's use of deceit and seduction to achieve her ends or the apparent acceptance of suicide under certain circumstances in 2 and 4 Maccabees. The representation of women in a number of these texts also presents significant challenges. In this chapter, we will explore the major contributions of the apocryphal books to ethics and examine some of the moral and patriarchal problems presented in the same.

Ethical Practices and Values Promoted in the Apocrypha

The Wisdom of Ben Sira (or "Sirach"), the longest book in the Apocrypha, is a collection of the instructions given in the decades surrounding 200 BCE by a Jerusalem sage to the youths of the Judean elite who were sent to him precisely for education in "instruction of manners." His purpose was to teach them how to live advantageously in the society of God and of other human beings. It comes as no surprise, therefore, that his work is a primary source for Jewish ethical practice in the period between the Testaments. The runner-up among the apocryphal books in the category of "most interested in ethics," however, is a fictional story. The author of Tobit combines edifying instruction with delightful narrative, teaching his audience through the example and the speech of his characters, affirming the value of their ethical practices through the flow of the narrative: their virtue causes God to take notice of them, and to deliver them from their respective plights. The entirety of the ethical instruction of these (and other) apocryphal texts occurs in the context of promoting commitment to the fear of the Lord and the doing of Torah as the core values of this life and as the path to a good future (Tob 4:5-6, 21; Sir 1:11-13), and of promoting obedience to God's Law as the source of true wealth and honor (Tob 4:21; 12:8; Sir 10:19-24; 40:26), as explored in the previous chapter.

1. Charity

The most prominent value promoted in the story of Tobit is charity toward the poor and the vulnerable. This is fully in line with the emphasis in the Torah and the Prophets on care for those in need: "You must open your hand generously to your fellow Israelites, to the needy among you, and to the poor who live with you in your land" (Deut 15:11). Tobit demonstrates this value throughout his life. When he resided in Israel, he diligently set aside the first tenth of his produce for the support of the Temple, but also the second tenth for distribution to "orphans and widows, and to Gentiles who had joined Israel" (Tob 1:7-8). In exile, he continued to support his relatives and other Israelites in exile as they had need, sharing his table with the poor (Tob 1:3; 2:2-3; 14:2), and he buried the exposed bodies of Israelites who had been murdered or executed and "flung outside the wall of Nineveh" (1:17). Acts of kindness toward the dead were considered the perfect act of charity, as there was no way for the doer to be rewarded by the recipient. Such was Tobit's commitment to charity that he persisted in these practices at great risk to himself, eventually fleeing as an enemy of the state (1:19-20).

What Tobit practices he also preaches. In what he thinks will be his final instructions to his son Tobias, Tobit gives almsgiving a prominent place:

> To everyone who practices righteousness, make donations based on what you have, and don't let your eye begrudge what you've given. Don't turn your face away from any poor person, and God's face will never turn away from you. Give aid, my child, according to what you have. If you have a lot, make a donation out of your riches. If you have only a little, don't be afraid to make

a donation in proportion. In this way, you will store up a valuable treasure for a time of need. Giving assistance to the poor rescues a person from death and keeps a person from going down into darkness. For everyone who does it, donating money to the needy is a good gift in the sight of the Most High. (Tob 4:7-11)

Giving to those in need is promoted as the most intelligent investment one can make now against an uncertain future. The cultural value of reciprocity probably undergirds this reasoning. In a moral universe, beneficence cannot go unrequited. Though the poor may not be able to reciprocate, God will requite in their own time of need those who have helped others in their time of need.[2] Such logic is solidly rooted in the wisdom tradition of Israel: "Those who are gracious to the poor lend to the LORD, and the Lord will fully repay them" (Prov 19:17). When the angel Raphael reveals himself to Tobit and his son, he also underscores the importance of the practice of charity, which is "better than storing up gold" because it "saves [the poor person] from death, and it washes away every sin" (Tob 12:8-9; see also Sir 3:30). It is Tobit's commitment to works of kindness that bring him to the notice of God's court, resulting in both his testing and God's decision to bring healing to his larger family and its line (12:12-14).

Like Tobit, Ben Sira also promotes care for the poor and disenfranchised through the sharing of material resources and other acts of kindness. Such deeds characterize the lives of "wise persons":

> Don't be timid in your prayer,
>   and don't neglect caring for those in need. . . .
> Extend your hand to the poor
>   so that your blessing may be complete.
> The kindness of a gift stands before all who are alive;
>   moreover, don't withhold kindness from the dead.
> Walk beside those who weep,
>   and mourn with those who mourn.
> Don't hesitate to visit the sick, because you will be loved on account
>   of these acts. (Sir 7:10, 32-35)

Charity is not just a matter of contributing, but of investing oneself in the lives of others where they are in need of some resource—material, emotional, relational—that one has to offer. The tears of the oppressed are pleas to God for vindication, and the God of justice will not fail to bring justice against those whose practices hurt the vulnerable (Sir 35:17-26). But the cry of the poor is also a danger to those who refuse to relieve their distress, for the poor person's curse against the heartless is also heard by God (Sir 4:3-5). Sins of omission are as grave as sins of commission. The wise will therefore reflect God's own heart for those in need (Sir 4:10) and invest their treasure "according to the commandments of the Most High," namely in relieving the need of others, for this becomes one's best defense against one's own future troubles (Sir 29:9-13).

Both Tobit and Ben Sira advise against giving to just anyone, but to limit the recipients of charity to the person who "pays attention to God with all his [or her] heart" (Tob 2:2) and to those who "practice righteousness," that is, live according to the Torah (Tob 4:7). Ben Sira is quite insistent:

> Do good to the godly, and you will find a reward,
> and if not from them, then from the Most High. . . .
> Give to the pious, but don't assist sinners.
> Do good to the humble, but don't give to the ungodly. . . .
> The Most High also hated sinners. . . .
> Give to good people, and don't assist sinners. (Sir 12:2, 4-7)

Ben Sira's rationales are twofold. First, virtuous people will not abuse charity; they will requite it if they can, and will certainly never harm the giver (Sir 12:2, 5). Second, God's favor rests on the pious, but not on those who are heedless of the commandments; human charity should reflect God's desire to benefit the former, but not the latter. Charity becomes another instrument for encouraging commitment to Torah observance, since shouldering up the covenant obligations makes one truly a part of the covenant community and, thus, part of its web of mutual assistance.

2. Duty Toward Kin

A second prominent value involves maintaining one's proper duty toward family. Foremost among these is a person's duty toward parents, in keeping with the fifth commandment of the Decalogue, "the first one with a promise attached" (Exod 20:12; Deut 5:16; Eph 6:2). Tobit instructs Tobias to honor his aging mother—Tobit's wife, Anna—taking care not to grieve her as long as she lives, as fair repayment for the pains she endured in carrying, giving birth to, and nurturing Tobias (Tob 4:3-4). When Tobias and Sarah marry, Sarah's father sends her to Tobias's household and declares Tobit and Anna to be her parents, just as surely as if they had conceived her themselves, and

Sarah's mother declares herself to be as fully Tobias's mother from that point on (10:12-13; see also 8:21). Tobias and Sarah care for both sets of aging parents as their own (14:13a). This is a vision for the relationship between in-laws very different from that promulgated in contemporary Western culture, affirming much more strongly how marriage unites two families as surely as blood and natural birth into a family unite kin.

Ben Sira devotes his third major piece of instruction to the debt of honor and care owed to parents. Giving attention, respect, and help to one's parents is, like almsgiving, compared to "storing up treasure" (Sir 3:4), this time a treasure that will be repaid in one's own old age by one's own children as well as by God (3:5). Ben Sira was aware of the trials of caring for the elderly, but regarded this as fitting repayment for the trials of bearing and caring for the young:

> My child, help your father in his old age,
>   and don't give him grief during his life.
> And if his understanding fails,
>   be tolerant,
>   and don't shame him,
>   because you have all your faculties.
> Taking care of one's father won't be forgotten.
>   It will be credited to you against your sins. . . .
> Those who abandon their fathers are like blasphemers,
>   and those who anger their mothers have been cursed by the Lord.
> (Sir 3:12-16)

Of course, the final duty toward parents involves providing for a proper burial after death (Tob 4:3a, 4b; 14:10a, 12-13a).

Ben Sira also teaches his students the importance of investing themselves in raising their own children, exercising the necessary discipline to help their sons and daughters internalize the core values that provide the foundation for an honorable and happy life (Sir 7:23; 16:1-4; 22:3-6; 30:1-13; 41:5-9). While we may blanch at his approval, indeed recommendation, of physical discipline, his fundamental concern that parents not neglect their duties in forming their children in virtue remains prophetic. Tobit and Anna provide living (if fictional) examples of proper childrearing in this regard, particularly in Tobit's commitment to modeling *and* teaching moral values to his son. These texts continue to challenge modern, Western cultures in regard to our deteriorating intergenerational connections and responsibility, both in regard to parents' personal investment in training their children and in regard to the relegation of the aging to the margins of home and society.

The duty of kin to prove reliable allies and sources of assistance extends beyond the immediate relationships of parents and children. In Tobit, Ahikar is presented as Tobit's nephew, and on this basis "naturally" helps Tobit both as advocate before the court of Esarhaddon and, when Tobit becomes blind, as provider (1:21-22; 2:10). Tobias and Tobit extend trust to the angel Raphael on the basis of the latter presenting himself as their kinsman Azariah. Since he is a relative, and since his "father" Hananiah diligently observed the Law alongside Tobit, he can be presumed to be a trustworthy companion for Tobias on his journey (5:9-14). By contrast, the treachery of Nadab against his uncle Ahikar is all the more heinous as his self-interested plot is pursued at the expense of a kinsman and benefactor (14:10-11). Essentially, cooperation and not competition ought to regulate all interactions between kin: competition is appropriate between people who are "outsiders" to one another, but kin are expected to put one another's interests and the overall advancement of the good of the larger family ahead of personal advancement at the expense of a family member.

3. Endogamy: Marrying Within the Jewish People

A third prominent value promoted particularly by Tobit is endogamy, the practice of marrying within one's kinship group or tribe. Tobit himself had married a kinswoman (Tob 1:9); Sarah's husbands had all been relatives from her father's family. When that circle was exhausted, she presumed herself to be out of options (3:15). Such a practice was particularly important during the period of Israel's occupation of the land, addressing the concern that the lands allotted to a particular tribe remain within that tribe (see Num 36:1-9). Since Sarah will inherit Raguel's estate, she is expected to marry within her father's ancestral tribe. This concern would have faded in exile and thereafter, but Tobit continues to promote the narrower understanding of endogamy perhaps in anticipation of Israel being restored to its ancestral holdings (4:12b; 13:5; 14:5), and perhaps in order to motivate readers *at least* to marry within Israel by praising the extreme.

It is striking that Tobit regards marriage with a non-Jewish woman to be a form of "fornication": "Child, keep yourself away from all inappropriate sex. First, take a wife from the descendants of your ancestors, and don't take a foreign woman who isn't from your ancestral tribe, for we are children of the prophets" (Tob 4:12a).

Not every marriage is licit in the sight of God, according to this author, beginning with marriages between Jews and non-Jews. This reflects (and underscores) the importance of genealogy for determining the constituency and the boundaries of Israel, the covenant people, also expressed in 1 Esdras and Ezra–Nehemiah (see 1 Esd 5:4-40). The importance of the purity of the "holy seed" that is Israel found its most dramatic, and no doubt heart-wrenching, expression in the dismissal of non-Jewish wives (among whose company may have been many Jewish women descended from those who remained in the land, who simply could not demonstrate their pedigree) *and* the children arising from those unions (1 Esd 8:65-67, 89-91).

Particularly in the Diaspora, intermarriage with non-Jews would have presented certain advantages, not least of which would be the benefits of closer integration into the dominant, empowered class, whether the local elite or the Greek overlords. Assimilation of conquered peoples through intermarriage, moreover, was a policy promoted by Alexander (who led by example in his marriage to Roxana) and followed by his soldiers. It is not in vain, therefore, that the author depicts Tobit urging his son to "love your relatives" and not to be "too proud in your heart to take a daughter from the descendants of your people as your wife" (Tob 4:13). Reinforcing endogamy, at least at the ethnic if not tribal level, was critical to maintaining Jewish identity in the Greek and Hellenistic world.[3]

Social Ethics and Etiquette

As a teacher preparing students to live wisely and virtuously in the everyday world of relationships and associations, Ben Sira gives significant attention to social ethics, incidentally bearing witness to several important facets of the ethos of the period. He trains his students to negotiate wisely the relationships forged by the giving and receiving of benefits, namely the relationships of patrons and clients and the relationships of friends. In preindustrial societies like ancient Rome, Greece, and Judea, "who you knew" really was vital for gaining access to goods, assistance, opportunities for advancement, protection, and the like. A person would meet another's need motivated by the willingness to do him or her a favor, and the recipient would seek to make a grateful return in some form, whether returning a favor someday if he or she were positioned to do so, or offering the giver honor and services if he or she lived on a lower sociopolitical level.[4] Gratitude is a necessary response to those by whom one has benefited and been supported (Sir 29:15-17). Such exchanges of favor tended to form relationships that could span generations, as Ben Sira indicates when he speaks of children repaying the kindnesses of their father's friends (30:6). Ben Sira also advises people to bestow their favors on virtuous people, who understand the value of reciprocity and will not take advantage of a person's favor (12:1-2). He warns similarly against accepting favors from ill-bred people who give gifts with a view to what they might get in return rather than out of a truly generous disposition (20:14-17).[5] Ben Sira is also aware that patronage and reciprocity can be perverted, as when a person uses a judge's obligations of gratitude to him or her to subvert justice, pressuring the judge for a favorable verdict for that person's clients or friends (19:25). He urges giving with a generous heart as well as hand, not mingling gifts with reproaches (18:15-18). Generosity toward particular individuals and toward the community at large is the path to an honorable reputation (31:23-24). Gratitude is always due God, the ultimate Benefactor of all. Giving God honor, service, and the offerings due to his ministers maintains the cycle of favor with the most important of patrons (35:12-13).

Ben Sira also gives attention to training in social etiquette, particularly in connection with the "symposium," a social gathering around wine tasting, conversation, music, and other entertainments. While the Greeks may be said to have perfected the symposium, such "wine parties" were indigenous to many Eastern cultures as well. First, Ben Sira teaches moderation in regard to food and drink (Sir 31:25-31; see also Tob 4:15). One shows one's good breeding by not allowing one's own desires for gobbling up delicacies to get in the way of sociable good feelings. The primary goal in attending a banquet should be to preserve the image of oneself as a considerate guest by manifesting self-control and by putting the enjoyment of the company ahead of self-indulgence:

> Don't reach out your hand for whatever you see,
>   and don't crowd your dinner companion by reaching into
>   the same bowl.
> Put yourself in your companion's place,
>   and be considerate in everything. (Sir 31:14-15)

Part of being a well-bred guest involves knowing the right time for the right activities and respecting social convention. Serious arguments are out of place after the third course of wine. Reproaching one's fellow in the midst of a party spoils everyone's fun. Drawing attention to oneself by talking while others are trying to listen to the musicians is rude.

Ben Sira promotes the virtue of prudence not only in social settings but also in more politically charged settings. This comes through in his "ethics of caution,"[6] an orientation shared by Egyptian and Greek sages. Gaining honor and influence in the ancient world almost inevitably meant rubbing shoulders with those who enjoyed greater honor and power than oneself—people who could make or break the upward climber (Sir 9:13; 13:8-13)—and jockeying for advancement in competition against others. Ben Sira sought in no way to deter his pupils from these endeavors, but warned them against falling along the way. He thus places a great deal of value on forethought (18:19-29; 38:18-23) and wisdom, shown by not entering battles one cannot win (8:1-2, 12, 14).

A critical aspect of survival in society involved sound household management and "economics" in the larger sense. He taught his students to be allergic to debt: "Those who build their houses with another person's money are like those who gather stones for their own burial mound" (Sir 21:8). His advice to minimize rather than accumulate debt is timeless, as many families have come to discover, laboring under their mortgages and other payments. He cautions maintaining financial independence as long as one is alive, not giving others control over one's estate or oneself until after death (33:20-24). Another timely word concerns striking a balance between the pursuits necessary for establishing a secure financial base and the enjoyment of life rather than letting life pass one by in the process (11:10-19; 14:3-19; 22:1-2; 40:28-30). And since Ben Sira teaches the Judean elite in his school, he gives attention to economic justice, including the command not to withhold a worker's wages, since those wages may be all that stand between a worker's family and hunger (Sir 34:27, in line with Lev 19:13; see also Tob 4:14).

Political Ethics

Texts written later in the Hellenistic and early Roman periods introduce another dimension to the ethical reflection in this corpus. Wisdom of Solomon, for example, presents itself in the first instance as an address to those "who judge the earth," urging them to do "what is right" (Wis 1:1). Pride in one's power is especially dangerous in the powerful: one's tendency to abuse power is indirectly proportional to one's sense of accountability to higher powers. Thus this author promotes humility among the powerful, urging them to regard themselves as stewards of God's power, entrusted to them as long as they "judge rightly, . . . keep the Law," and "act according to God's plan" (6:4). God, the most powerful of all, will hold political rulers to a strict account: "Judgment falls hard on those in high places. . . . A stern judgment will fall upon the ruthless" (6:5, 8).

Jews were in a strong position to observe and experience colonization by another power, having been colonized by Assyria, Babylon, Greece, the Hellenistic kingdoms of Syria and Egypt, and finally Rome. While the colonizing power is sometimes portrayed positively, as when it empowers the resettlement of Jerusalem after the exile, most portraits found in the literature of the period depict "empires behaving badly," and some of these texts reflect in some detail on the unethical practices of colonizing powers. The author of 4 Ezra (2 Esd 3–14), an apocalypse written several decades after Rome's suppression of the Jewish Revolt and destruction of the Temple in 70 CE, looks forward to the intervention of a Messiah who will hold Rome accountable for these practices. The messianic lion is roused at last, upbraiding the eagle-monster of Rome for

> ruling over the world with much terror and over the whole world with harsh oppression. You have lived in the world with deceit for so long! You judged the earth, but not in truth, for you have oppressed the meek and injured those who caused no unrest. You hated those who spoke the truth and loved liars. You destroyed the dwellings of those who bore fruit and tore down the walls of those who had done you no harm. Your insolence has ascended to the Most High and your pride to the mighty one. . . . Therefore, eagle, you must utterly vanish. . . . Then the whole earth will be refreshed and restored, set free from your violence, and will hope for the judgment and mercy of him who made it. (2 Esd 11:40-43, 45-46)

The author names several of the unethical practices of Rome in its imperialistic expansion and its maintenance of its empire, not least of which is its exercise of destructive force against peaceful, neighboring states. Rome was willing that many people who had given Rome no provocation should die, that the delicate balance of economies of subsistence agriculture be shattered with ruinous consequences for the indigenous people, all for the sake of expanding its control, power, and, eventually, wealth.

The author also underscores Rome's response to truth-telling and its opposite. Speech is an important tool in such encounters between colonizing power and colonized people. The lion is a truth-teller; others have told the truth about Roman domination before him. Rome has not listened, so as to engage in salutary self-examination, but has sought to silence critical voices as threats to the security and peace of its empire. On the other hand, Rome has rewarded those who, by their speech, have advanced Rome's interest, legitimated Rome's presence, whitewashed the "unfortunate" things Rome has had to do to bring stability and peace to the *orbis terrarum*, the circle of the lands around the Mediterranean Sea, the center of the world. Hope for the "kingdom of God" is fueled throughout this period by the regular experience of the underside of imperialism.

While couched as an essay on the ability of the Torah-trained mind to master the emotions, drives, and sensations that potentially lead the individual person away from virtuous practices, 4 Maccabees also addresses issues of political ethics and the ethics of resistance to a colonizing power. Arrogance is the major political vice that the author identifies in those who represent empire, typified here by Antiochus IV. The practices of empire exhibit what the author calls "the arrogant logic of tyranny" (4 Macc 9:30, author's translation). This arrogance appears in the colonizing power's failure to exercise itself to understand the inherent reasonableness and integrity of the way of life of the subjugated culture, labeling it instead as deficient. Such labeling makes it easier for the colonizer to impose changes on that way of life, regarding it as remediation or improvement (5:5-13; 8:5-11). The ultimate argument undergirding "the arrogant logic of tyranny" is the colonizer's power over the bodies of the colonized, the ability to "persuade" by inflicting pain and death (5:6, 13; 8:6, 9, 11).

In the face of the imposition of a foreign way of life, the author advocates an ethic of resistance. Resistance begins where the colonized refuse to accept the colonizer's negative assessment of their way of life, but rather continue to value their distinctive culture and develop rationales for continuing to adhere to the same. Eleazar demonstrates this response as he rejects the claim that living in alignment with Torah is "unreasonable" (4 Macc 5:22), explaining that Jews attain the very same moral ideals prized by the colonizing power by following their ancestral way of life:

> Our way of life teaches us self-control, so that we can have control over any pleasure or desire. It trains us to be brave, so that we willingly bear any suffering. It educates us about justice, so that it is always our custom to treat everyone fairly. It educates us in the godly way of life, so that we worship with due respect the only God who really exists. (4 Macc 5:23-24)

Self-control, bravery, justice, and piety were, of course, principal virtues in Greek systems of ethics as well.

Such a posture, in turn, ennobles resistance in body. The real shame for Eleazar is not the degrading treatment to which he is subjected by the tyrant's soldiers, but violating his own moral integrity by abandoning his people's way of life and giving greater impetus to assimilation among those who view his own capitulation (4 Macc 5:29-38; 6:18-19, 22). As we observed already in regard to 4 Ezra, resistance takes place also in the speech of the colonized, as they challenge the aggressive behaviors of the colonizer and stir up commitment to the ancestral way of life among their people (4 Macc 6:17-22; 13:13-18; 16:16-23). The martyrs exhibit the virtuous practice of *parrhesia,* "bold speech" (10:5). This was a practice prized in Greek democratic societies and was especially valued where tyranny threatened to replace democracy. Speaking truth to power incurs tremendous risks and requires courage, but it is required if the moral integrity of the subordinate is to be preserved. It also offers potentially reformative critique to those in power, inviting them to self-examination as they hear the witness of the subordinate to their injustice (9:15; 10:10; 11:4-6; 12:11-14). This is most strongly exemplified in the speech of the seventh and last brother:

> You unholy tyrant! . . . You received your kingdom and all good things from God. So why have you felt no shame for murdering God's servants and torturing the champions of the godly way of life? . . . As a human being weren't you ashamed [to] cut out the tongues and abuse and torture people who have feelings just like you and who are made of the same flesh and blood as you[?] (4 Macc 12:11, 13)

The author, in the person of the martyr, chastens the powerful for allowing the lines that create an "us" and a "them," a "colonizer" and a "colonized," to obscure the common bond of humanity that binds both parties together, and therefore to lose sight of the necessity of pursuing humane practices even in the midst of imperial domination. The same God looks down upon both colonizer and colonized, and holds both accountable to values of humaneness that transcend national interests or agendas.

The author suggests, in the end, that the preservation of the freedom of one's moral faculty in a situation of domination, where security comes at the cost of moral integrity, impels one to such acts of resistance. These questions were not merely of historical interest in regard to the period prior to the Maccabean Revolt: they were, to one degree or another, relevant throughout the period of Hellenistic and Roman domination, whether in Judea or, all the more, living in the western Diaspora.

Ethical Problems Identified by, and in, the Apocryphal Books

1. Losing Sight of Eternity

The author of Wisdom of Solomon opens the body of his work by identifying a major hindrance to maintaining ethical practices. He frames this as losing sight of eternity, the larger purposes of God for humanity (Wis 1:12-15; 2:22-23). The people at risk are those who look at death as the end of their existence, for whom the impetus to get all the good things for oneself that one can in this life is thereby magnified. As a result, their entire system of values is grossly distorted. Their inability to see any reason to live beyond themselves results in their commitment to try to fill their emptiness with temporal pleasures:

> Come then! Let's enjoy all the good things of life now. Let's enjoy creation to the fullest as we did in our youth. Let's drink our fill of expensive wines and enjoy fine perfumes. Let's pluck every fresh blossom of spring as we pass by. Let's crown ourselves with rosebuds before they wither. Let's make sure that no meadow is left untouched by our high-spirited fun. Let's leave evidence everywhere that we made the most of this life, because this life is all we have. (Wis 2:6-9)[7]

Those whose primary value has become self-gratification—the fulfillment of their own interests—quickly lose sight of any moral obligation to safeguard the interests of others, particularly those who are weaker and whose resources, therefore, could be co-opted to serve the more powerful person's lust for gratification:

> Let's take advantage of the day laborer who does what's right. Let's not be afraid to abuse the widow. Let's show that we couldn't care less for the gray hair of our elders. May strength be our only law and determine what's right, for it's clear to us that what is weak is worthless. (2:10-11)

In losing sight of their accountability before God (a major ethical consideration upheld by beliefs in an afterlife), the "ungodly" have lost their ethical moorings. These individuals have seen that Torah observance is not the only, and often not even the best, path to attain the good things of this life that the covenant promises. This is increasingly true under foreign domination and, all the more, in Diaspora. They have abandoned the values instilled in their training (presumably in Torah; Wis 2:12b), and have instead become agents of the moral chaos that pervades society when self-interest and self-gratification become the highest values.

The author therefore underscores the conviction that God's purposes for humankind extend beyond this life, that the experience of death is not the final word, and, therefore, the advantage of keeping covenant with God is not to be judged solely (or even primarily) on the basis of whether or not it leads to the enjoyment of greater goods in *this* life than other ways of life. People who make their ethical decisions in this way "didn't know of God's secret plan. They didn't hope for the reward that holiness brings. They didn't consider the prize they would win if they kept their whole beings free from stain. God created humans to live forever" (Wis 2:22-23). The author creates vivid scenes of the encounter with God beyond death, in which the person who has kept his or her moral compass fixed on God's values is rewarded with honor in God's presence, and in which those who have put considerations of self-interest above regard for God and for neighbor will confess their error in shame and confusion (3:1-9; 5:1-16). In this way, the author affirms that living in line with God's values—and thus not violating the neighbor in any way to advance one's own aims in *this* life—remains the ethical mandate for living with integrity here and hereafter.

2. Feminine Virtue

The stories of the Apocrypha, together with the Wisdom of Ben Sira, give significant attention to ethical ideals for women, as well as ethical problems allegedly connected with women.

Foremost among virtues promoted for women is sexual continence, abstinence from any sexual activity outside of marriage, with a marked preference for having sex with only one partner throughout all of life. In the story of Tobit, Sarah pleads her innocence in God's sight primarily in terms of her chastity, such that she should not have to endure taunts from any person (3:14-15). Both Judith and the mother of the seven martyred brothers—exemplars of so many other virtues—must also affirm their chastity prior to marriage and sexual fidelity to one man *and* his memory (Jdt 8:2, 4; 13:16; 16:22; 4 Macc 18:7-9). Ben Sira is almost obsessive in his concern with a woman's sexual virtue and in his fear that a woman will not maintain her virtue. He especially underscores the importance of watching over daughters so as to safeguard their virginity against their own assumed inclinations (Sir 7:24; 26:10-12; 42:9-12).

This focus on female sexuality and chastity is a reflection of the cultural dynamics in the ancient Mediterranean world—dynamics shared by Greek, Roman, Jewish, and multiple other indigenous societies. A woman was not seen as an independent entity, but rather as embedded somehow in a male. Before marriage, she would be, in effect, an extension of her father; after marriage, she would be an extension of her husband. The responsible male was charged with the preservation of the sexual purity or exclusivity of the females in his household. Their sexuality, therefore, was a point at which his honor was constantly vulnerable. If his wife or daughter were found to have had illicit sex, *he* would become, in Ben Sira's words, "an object of ridicule to [his] enemies, a topic of talk in the city and the assembly of the people" (Sir 42:11). A daughter was, in such a culture, a potential threat to a father's honor, even after marriage, hence Ben Sira's harsh claim: "a daughter's birth is a liability" (22:3). In practice, of course, a daughter's character would determine whether or not her birth was a liability or a great credit, and Ben Sira has been justly criticized over the millennia for consigning all daughters to the debit column. In general, Ben Sira shares with ethicists from multiple locations in the ancient Mediterranean (from Aristotle to Plutarch) a configuration of feminine virtues that exhibits and maintains the woman's subordination to male authority—hence underscoring silence (or the absence of disagreeable speech), obedience, and modesty (Sir 25:20, 25-26; 26:14-15, 24-27).[8]

While the other authors of the apocryphal books do not overturn this portrait, they do offer some important counterpoints. First, women are quite visible in many of the narratives. The books of Tobit, Judith, and 4 Maccabees are concerned just as fully with women as with the male characters in the same. God has regard both for Tobit and for Sarah as God sends his angel to answer the prayers of both (Tob 3:16-17). The author showcases Anna's love for her son and her nobility of spirit, preferring to forgo recovering their life savings rather than put Tobias in harm's way (Tob 5:18-20). Tobit's virtue is a testimony to his grandmother Deborah, who raised him after he was orphaned (Tob 1:8). Second, while patriarchy is not itself questioned, these texts promote an ethic of marriage as a process of mutual adaptation (Sir 25:1) that can bring great joy (Sir 26:1-4), and as a partnership that cannot make the spouse the vehicle for sexual gratification nor become a source of grief for the woman, the more vulnerable party (Tob 8:5-7; 10:12).

More strikingly, however, two of these texts—Judith and 4 Maccabees— show women breaking out of conventional roles at a number of points and, indeed, exhibiting greater virtue and achievements than males. Judith is the head of her deceased husband's household (Jdt 8:7; 16:21, 24b). She summons the city's elders to her house and chides them for acquiescing to pressures to surrender the city. Even though this meeting does take place in the private spaces of her home (rather than the city gate), Judith is hardly the picture of silence and submissiveness (Jdt 8:9-27). These same elders entrust her with delivering the city, which she accomplishes, of course, by using her feminine wiles to seduce the invading general in order to get close enough to kill him. She even replaces Joakim as the military commander, giving the instructions for the city's attack on Holofernes's camp (14:1-5).

Granted that Judith is domesticated once more at the story's conclusion, returning to the life of a private citizen and celibate widow,[9] her story suggests that women can accomplish great things for God on behalf of God's people, particularly when men fail to step forward. She also demonstrates, against Ben Sira, that "a daughter's birth" is not necessarily a "liability" (Sir 22:3), since she put her (fictional) father, Merari, on the map of national memory as no son did. Her example of chastity—even though perfectly capable of using her looks and charms to seduce—is similarly a statement about a woman's ability to master her own sexual passions, even while the foreigner Holofernes was unable to exhibit such self-control. Where the male elders vacillated in weakness, Judith provided definitive and effective leadership. She does not create a new space for herself (or, thus, women) in the public sphere, but she does represent the author's estimation of women's potential and the author's suspicion of cultural assumptions about men's natural superiority.

3. Judith and the Ethics of Deceit

In the book of Judith, the heroine's strategy for delivering her city and, ultimately, Judea from the armies of Holofernes involves—indeed, centers upon—deceit. She lies to Holofernes and his soldiers about conditions in Bethulia, even as she swears to be telling them the truth (Jdt 11:5). She says that the people are about to eat the portions of food that had been collected as tithes sacred to the Temple, though they are planning no such thing, and that God will therefore overthrow the city within a matter of days (11:10-15). She further lies to them about her intentions as she goes outside the enemy camp each night to purify herself in a stream and to pray, posing as a prophetess to whom God would reveal her people's transgression, so that she can tell Holofernes, in turn, when it is time for his troops to attack (11:17-19; 12:6-9). In reality, she is establishing a pattern that will allow her to escape the camp after murdering the general (13:8-10). She even asks God to use her "lying lips" as the means by which to bring about his deliverance of his people (9:10, 13). Throughout the story, she appears to relish in ambiguous speech, which is also part of her attempt to deceive (11:6, 16; 12:4, 14, 18). Part of her deceit involves, of course, leading Holofernes on to think that he will have his way with her before she leaves his camp (12:14–13:2).

These facets of the story have often provoked criticism of Judith's ethical integrity. At best, readers may have been willing to allow that "all's fair in love and war" or that "the end justifies the means" when under such duress as Judith's people found themselves.[10] There was, however, an ethical place for deceit in interactions in the ancient world, particularly where deceit could help advance the interests of, or preserve the honor of, oneself or one's primary reference group against the assaults of outsiders on those interests or that honor. Knowledge is a commodity; knowledge in the wrong hands can be used against oneself or one's circle of significant others. Therefore, a person has no obligation to give truthful knowledge to those who are seeking to gain honor or advance their interests at his or her expense, any more than one is obliged to give a weapon to an enemy.[11]

Knowledge of the truth is owed only to members of one's group (whether family, circle of associates, or nation), who will not use such knowledge against the giver. When one's group's honor or security is threatened, deceit is one of many acceptable strategies by means of which one may seek to minimize harm or even gain the upper hand against the outside threat.[12] An outstanding example of this comes from Greek history, when the Athenian Themistocles lures the Persian fleet commanders to their defeat by pretending to form an alliance with them against the other Greek city-states and by providing false intelligence reports (Thucydides, *Hist.* 8.75–90). The honors awarded Themistocles bear witness to the acceptability of deceit as a weapon against outsiders. It is the latter's responsibility not to be duped; if he or she is, he or she is the one who is put to shame.

Judith appropriately uses all of the strategies available to her in order to answer multiple challenges to her honor and the honor of those whom she represents. First and foremost of these is Holofernes' challenge to the honor of the God of Israel, as the general affirms the divinity of his human master, Nebuchadnezzar, and seeks to suppress every local cult of another god in favor of ruler cult (Jdt 3:8). Holofernes' challenge, "Who is god except Nebuchadnezzar?" (6:2), must be answered by the one true God and his followers. Indeed, Judith is particularly concerned that God's honor be vindicated in this situation (9:14), giving herself over to God as the instrument for the same. The hollowness of Holofernes' boasts would be demonstrated when the One God defeated Holofernes' mighty army "by the hand of a woman" (9:9-14; 16:5-6). A second honor challenge involves the sexually charged interactions between Holofernes and Judith. Judith's presence in the camp is an implicit challenge to Holofernes, who thinks it will be a disgrace to him if he fails to conquer Judith sexually (12:13). He seeks to seduce her not only for the sake of pleasure, but for the sake of preserving his reputation as a virile male.[13] This is, of course, a direct challenge to Judith's honor as well, which is most closely bound to her chastity.

Judith defeats Holofernes because he fails to remain master of himself. He fails to maintain a healthy suspicion toward an outsider who promised to betray her own to strangers. He acts without prudence in the presence of one of the enemy, and allows intemperance to rob him of his wits at the critical moment. His lack of self-mastery leaves him unable to defend himself like a man, such that he is indeed disgraced "by the hand of a woman"—and Nebuchadnezzar's entire house is disgraced as well, even as God's honor is vindicated (Jdt 13:17; 14:18). Judith did not violate contemporary ethics by pursuing her stratagem. The commandment against bearing false witness is a word to safeguard the integrity of the internal judicial processes of Israel, not a commandment against withholding truth from outsiders to protect Israel and its honor. Rather, Judith exhibited the utmost integrity between the piety she practiced in the tent upon her own roof and the course she pursued in Holofernes' tent.

4. The Ethics of Suicide

The Apocrypha are frequently criticized by those who argue against their inspiration or canonicity for commending suicide. There are, however, very few instances of suicide in these texts, and those that are recounted—indeed without rebuke—happen under very peculiar circumstances of colonial oppression. In 2 Maccabees, the Jewish elder Razis is hunted out by the Syrian general Nicanor with malicious intent. When he was finally surrounded in a tower that would not long withstand the siege, he "fell on his own sword. He wanted to die bravely rather than fall into the hands of sinners and suffer outrages unworthy of his own high birth" (2 Macc 14:41-42). While the same author indicates that all seven of the brothers and their mother died under torture, the author of 4 Maccabees purposefully changes this narrative. The seventh brother, after denouncing the tyrant in no uncertain terms, "threw himself into the container of burning coal and so gave back his life" (4 Macc

12:19). Similarly, in the case of the mother, "some of the guards reported that, just as they were about to grab the mother and put her to death as well, she threw herself into the fire before anyone could touch her body" (4 Macc 17:1). In every instance, the death of the individual was inevitable. Taking the manner of that death out of the hands of the oppressing party was the only means by which to preserve personal honor, forestalling degrading treatment in the form of either torture or sexual assault. It was the only way to seize back a modicum of power over one's own body in an otherwise impossible situation of personal violation.

Notably, suicide is not pursued in these texts as a way out of more mundane personal trials. Despair does not lead Tobit and Sarah, for example, to take their own lives, but only to pray to God for release from life (Tob 3:6, 13, 15c). Sarah, indeed, explicitly repents of her plan to hang herself, and thus find release from her predicament, because of the pain this would bring those who would survive her (Tob 3:10). It is unfair, therefore, to characterize these texts as ethically suspect; rather, they deal with ethical issues in all their complexity, avoiding hard-and-fast positions when the range of human experience requires a range of responses in regard to an ethical problem like suicide.

Chapter 5

The Apocrypha and Jewish Spirituality

For the Jews who wrote and read the texts in the Apocrypha, the concept of "piety" encompassed much more than the range of activities that we might tend to associate with the word. "Piety" included observing the Torah in all of its particulars, including those areas that we might classify as "ethical" rather than "religious" matters. For the Jew, however, these were *all* religious matters, as they were all embedded in the relationship between the One God and the people called by that God to be his special possession among the nations.

The spirituality of keeping the covenant as a whole is evident, for example, in the ways in which these authors speak about "Wisdom," which becomes a relational figure rather than an object of human knowledge.

> Wisdom is the warm breath of God's power. She pours forth from the all-powerful one's pure glory. Therefore, nothing impure can enter her. She's the brightness that shines forth from eternal light. She's a mirror that flawlessly reflects God's activity. She's the perfect image of God's goodness. She can do anything, since she's one and undivided. She never changes, and yet she makes everything new. Generation after generation, she enters holy beings and shapes them into God's friends and prophets. God doesn't love anything as much as people who make their home with Wisdom. (Wis 7:25-28)

"Wisdom" is seen as a part of God that can become a part of the human being: it proceeds from God, enters into humans, and knits them together in a relationship of "friendship." This connection is a matter of "keep[ing] her laws" (Wis 6:18), ordering one's steps day by day in alignment with the

Torah, where Wisdom becomes Word (Sir 24:3-23; Bar 3:9–4:4). Knowing and doing what pleases God, and knowing that one is doing this, is an essential point of connection with God, and thus a critical component of the spirituality of this period.

As we have focused on these facets of piety, however, in the previous two chapters, here we will explore the dimensions of the Apocrypha that tend to fall within the parameters of "spirituality" or "religious practice," such as the practices of prayer, worship, and ritual. The apocryphal books are replete with prayer, in some instances *more* than we find in the canonical Scriptures. The expanded versions of Greek Daniel and Esther are both richer than their Hebrew and Aramaic counterparts in this regard (hence, also richer than the versions found in the Protestant Old Testament). Introducing new prayers into the story of Esther exemplifies the importance of centering oneself on God and invoking God's help, the importance of reinforcing one's connection with God before critical events, for the editors and readers of Greek Esther. Introducing hymns of praise into the story of the three Judeans in the fiery furnace exemplifies the importance of acknowledging God's generous interventions in human experience, meeting the needs of those who petition him. And if the books of the New Testament witness to a Jewish movement in which the importance of the liturgical calendar of Judaism and the cultic activity of the Temple is increasingly diminished in favor of new sacred times and spaces, the Apocrypha testify to the ongoing vitality of these holy days and rites for those who observe them.

Petition

Prayer allows individuals to tap into God's empowerment for challenging ventures, or to seek God's deliverance when circumstances are beyond the individual's power to affect or endure. Prayers for help are often grounded in what God has done for Israel in the past. A foundational premise in the "logic" of prayer seems to be that what God has done for Israel before, God can do again. Indeed, what God has done for Israel before reveals something of the values and character of God that, being constant, provides the ground for hope that God will intervene in similar ways again in situations that reflect similar dynamics.

Judas Maccabeus, the military hero of the revolt against Seleucid domination, prays before entering into battle. In an early prayer, he grounds his petition against the overwhelming forces surrounding his army by remembering how God "crushed the attack of the mighty warrior through the power of your servant David" and "handed over the camp of the Philistines to Saul's son Jonathan and the man who carried his armor" (1 Macc 4:30). As God allowed David to overcome the giant Goliath (1 Sam 17:4-54) and Jonathan and his armor-bearer to initiate an attack on the enemy camp (1 Sam 14:1-16), killing twenty themselves and putting the camp into a panic, God might be expected to bring victory again through the outnumbered and outmatched forces of his people. In a later episode, Judas mobilizes to respond to Nicanor's threat against the Temple. In his prayer, he remembers the similar threat of Sennacherib of Assyria against the Temple, when Sennacherib boasted that no other god had hitherto halted his advance, and God's vindication of God's honor by destroying 185,000 of Sennacherib's troops (2 Kgs 19:8-37). God's earlier defense of his honor, protecting his holy place, provides a foundation for the hope that God would do so in the present situation (given the renewal of zeal for the covenant that Judas and his family had catalyzed).

When Judith prays before leaving Bethulia for the enemy's camp, she also looks to Scripture as a resource for discovering paradigms of how God acts on behalf of and through people in new generations. She lights upon the story of Shechem's rape of Dinah in Genesis 34 and Simeon's response, using subterfuge and violence to avenge an assault on the honor of Israel. In Judith's situation, foreigners are making another such assault, this time not on the sanctity of a virgin, but on the sanctity of the Temple in God's Holy City. Knowing how God prospered her ancestor Simeon's plan, she prays that God would now use her to defend the honor and purity of God's Temple and people through her own stratagem of subterfuge and violence (Jdt 9:2-14).

Such a practice pervades Diaspora Jewish texts as well. Third Maccabees includes two lengthy prayers, one offered by the high priest Simon in the face of Ptolemy's determination to enter the Temple (3 Macc 2:2-20), and one offered by an Eleazar, an aged priest in Egypt, when the Jews of Egypt were on the brink of extermination (6:2-15). Simon establishes on the basis of three stories—those concerning the giants, Sodom, and Pharaoh (Gen 6:1-4; 19:1-29; Exod 3–15)—that God judges those who act arrogantly toward God's standards, people, or chosen city. By intervening in this way, God effectively answers the challenge to his honor offered by the arrogant, reestablishing his honor in the sight of the nations. On this basis, he asks God to intervene once more to safeguard the sanctity of the Temple. Eleazar focuses on God's deliverance of God's people from extinction when threatened by Pharaoh at the Red Sea (Exod 14) and by Sennacherib outside of Jerusalem (2 Kgs 19), and on God's deliverance of Daniel, Hananiah, Mishael, and Azariah in Babylon

(Dan 3; 6). As God so acted in the past when God's people were put at risk by an arrogant foreigner, Eleazar prays to God to intervene in their present distress.

All these prayers exemplify praying in line with what can be known about God, seeking to guard against expecting God to do something that is out of character or contrary to what God has revealed to be his intentions in the sacred tradition. This pattern of grounding one's prayer in an older revelation of God's character, purposes, and interventions continues long into both Jewish and Christian practice, observable, for example, in the cycle of collects prayed in the Catholic, Anglican, and Lutheran traditions. It remains a salutary example of the practice of praying in line with God's will, as opposed to offering frivolous prayers based solely on one's own wishes.

The books of the Apocrypha also express the conviction that God is concerned not just with the nation as a whole (or with issues of import for a large population), but with each individual in his or her particular plight. Thus we also find petitions offered on behalf of personal needs, as well as the expectation that God hears and makes provision for the same. Tobit, Sarah, and Tobias and Sarah together offer such prayers in the book of Tobit. Faced with the intolerability of their situations, both Tobit and Sarah seek God's deliverance. Their prayers recall the psalms of lament, save for the fact that the psalmists uniformly seek deliverance *from* death rather than asking *for* death as a means of release from their troubles. Both prayers also notably include some words of respect toward God, whether acknowledging God's justice (in Tobit's case, 3:2, 5) or the honor due God's name from all creation (in Sarah's case, 3:11). Both prayers exhibit a high level of honesty and openness before God, with both Tobit and Sarah speaking very plainly about their grievances and their desire for God's intervention.

The prayer of Tobias and Sarah on their wedding night is a particularly artistic example of a personal petition:

> "Blessed are you, God of our ancestors, and blessed is your name for all generations. May the heavens and all your creation bless you forever! You created Adam and you created Eve his wife to help and support him, and from the two of them has come the human race. You said, 'It isn't good for the man to be alone; let's make for him a helper like himself.' I'm not taking this sister of mine now out of lust but with honest integrity. Grant that she and I will be shown mercy and grow old together." (Tob 8:5-7)

Tobias begins his prayer, as did Tobit and Sarah, with a declaration of God's praise, acknowledging God's honor. He follows this by searching out the divine purposes that are at risk of being unfulfilled, and for the fulfillment of which he and Sarah are praying. In this particular prayer, he cites God's purposes for a man and a woman in marriage. He affirms that their purposes in marrying are, in fact, aligned with God's intentions for the same. Only after this does Tobias make his request, namely that they will survive the night and live to fulfill God's purposes in creation and in the institution of marriage with each other. Like the prayers in 1 Maccabees, Judith, and 3 Maccabees, this prayer models "praying according to God's will" also in regard to personal concerns. The petitioner considers *God's* own purposes first, embedding the request in the same insofar as it aligns with God's purposes.

The narrative context affirms that such prayers are effective. Notably, they are effective not strictly in terms of the petitioner's request, but in terms of God's generous provision for the petitioners (Tobit certainly gets something better than what he asks for, namely death). "The prayers of both Sarah and Tobit were heard in God's glorious presence," with the result that "Raphael was sent to heal the two of them" (Tob 3:16-17). Tobias and Sarah do enjoy a long and fulfilling marriage, the demon having been bound by Raphael after the exorcism (8:1-3). Indeed, the narrative affirms the connection between the various aspects of piety that we have been exploring: Tobit's wholehearted devotion to the covenant plays a role in God's disposition to resolve his family's particular needs and concerns (12:12-15).

Several of these texts affirm the importance of prayer as a means of discerning God's counsel. Ben Sira affirms that a person does not become wise only through study and conversation with the sages, but through giving significant time to prayer and conversation with the Source of all wisdom:

> They will commit themselves to rise early, to seek the Lord who made
> them,
> and to pray to the Most High.
> They will open their mouth in prayer and ask forgiveness for their sins.
> If the great Lord is willing, they will be filled with a spirit of understanding;
> they will pour forth words of wisdom,
> and they will give thanks to the Lord in prayer.
> Their reasoning and knowledge will remain on course,
> and they will ponder God's mysteries. (Sir 39:5-7)

Ben Sira affirms the importance of seeking out the counsel of those whose own interests do not conflict with one's own best interests, treasuring the counsel of Torah-observant people and trusting one's own intuition. The most reliable source of good counsel, however, remains God: "But above everything else, pray to the Most High, so that he may make your path straight in truth" (Sir 37:15). There is no room, however, for taking counsel through "divinations, omens, and dreams" (34:5), which are empty parodies of genuine spirituality. Ben Sira appears to have known from personal experience that one's own wisdom and circumspection are, in the end, never enough to guarantee security: deliverance, in the end, comes from God and is sought in prayer (51:1-12).

The author of 4 Ezra opens another window into the importance of prayer as an avenue for discernment and discovery of wisdom. As we have already seen, the figure of "Ezra" searches out answers to some of the pressing questions challenging Jews in the decades following Rome's devastation of Jerusalem and its Temple in 70 CE. Here it remains to notice that a person should not expect to discover such answers without wholehearted investment in the process of seeking God's face and waiting upon God's response. "Ezra" devotes entire weeks to fasting, solitude, and prayer—forty days in all in the course of the original Jewish apocalypse (2 Esd 3–14; see esp. 5:20; 6:35; 9:23-27)—not because it takes God that long to speak to human beings, but because it can take that long for human beings to discover what is at the heart of their concerns and to prepare themselves to hear from God. The authorial persona in this text also models the importance both of bringing what is truly on one's mind and heart before God in prayer *and* of not leaving the place of prayer without listening for God's response.

Ezra's example also highlights the embodied spirituality of Jews in this period. In many situations of prayer, one finds the ones praying changing their clothing and doing other things with and to their bodies expressive of humility and humiliation. When seeking God's help in a desperate situation, Esther "took off her royal garments and put on mourning clothes. Instead of the finest spices, she smeared her head and body with ashes and dung, and humbled herself" (Add Esth C:13). Judith lay down with her face to the ground, "put ashes on her head, and uncovered the funeral clothing she was wearing" (Jdt 9:1). The crowds of Jews seeking God's intervention on the Temple's behalf also prostrate themselves with their faces to the ground, sprinkle dust and ashes on their heads, and dress in rough fabric (2 Macc 3:15, 19, 21; 3 Macc 1:16, 18). These all evidence the practice of throwing one's whole being, and not just one's internal self, into prayer and seeking God's intervention.

Penitence

The Apocrypha contain several prayers seeking God's forgiveness for failure on the part of human beings to keep faith with God by living in alignment with the Torah. The Prayer of Manasseh offers such a prayer on behalf of the individual sinner; the Prayer of Azariah and Baruch 1:15–3:8 offer prayers on behalf of the nation that has alienated itself from God.

The Prayer of Manasseh is one of the liturgical highlights of the Apocrypha. It begins by acknowledging God's power and righteousness evident in creation, and the threat such power poses to those who provoke God's anger by sinning against God's Law (Pr Man 1-5). But, the author declares, this same God is "kind, patient, and merciful," compassionate toward the sorrows that come upon humans, even when deserved (v. 7). This is the language of God's revelation of himself to Moses in Exodus 34:6: "a God who is compassionate and merciful, very patient." Hope for the sinner is thus found in one of the most powerful moments of God's self-revelation in the Scriptures.

Because of God's character as both just *and* merciful, sinners have the opportunity, provided by God, to change their hearts and minds—in traditional language, to "repent." Acknowledging what one has done wrong and expressing heartfelt sorrow for the consequences this has brought to one's life and one's relationship with God allow the sinner to find a point of connection with the "God of those who do what is right" (Pr Man 8). The prayer is especially reminiscent of Psalm 51, the classic prayer of repentance in the Hebrew Bible, as the author acknowledges his error and the justice of God's sentence, and asks God for mercy and restoration to relationship.

The author asks for forgiveness using a beautiful image of humility: "Now I bend the knee of my heart, begging you to show kindness" (Pr Man 11, author's trans.). The author affirms that his outward posture of a suppliant on his knees is the exterior reflection of the attitude of his inner being toward God. The arrogance that he showed when he disregarded God's laws is gone, and he has returned to a proper attitude before the Life-giver. He affirms that the same God who is "God of those who do what is right" (v. 8) is also "God of those who turn from their sins" (v. 13). The God who created all persons does not cease to be the God of those who fail in their obligations toward God, but stands ready to forgive and restore those who humble themselves and change their lives. Restoration of the sinner reveals God's honor in the world, showing his generous nature (v. 14). Notably, the author promises to contribute to extending this honor through testimony to God's goodness, thus showing his gratitude and acknowledging his debt to God (v. 15).

The Prayer of Azariah is a petition for forgiveness and restoration for the people as a whole. The author opens the prayer with a particular form:

> Blessed are you, Lord God of our ancestors.
> You deserve to be praised and honored forever! (Pr Azar 3)

This "benediction" form pervades the prayers in this literature (Tob 3:11; 8:5, 15, 16, 17; 11:14; 13:1, 17; Jdt 13:17; Pr Azar 1:29; 1 Macc 4:30; 2 Macc 1:17; 1 Esd 3:40, 60; 3 Macc 7:23) and probably reflects a broader practice of opening prayers to God in this manner, as well as the practice of using this form to acknowledge benefits received from God.

As with the prayers of confession in Baruch 1:1–3:8 and Daniel 9:4-19, this prayer begins by acknowledging that God has acted with fairness and justice, living up to God's word in Deuteronomy. It is Israel that is to blame for failing God, and not the reverse. The author confesses the nation's faithlessness in regard to living by the covenant, but holds on to the hope of restoration. In addition to the promises of Deuteronomy in this regard, the author urges God to be reconciled with God's penitent people for the sake of the promises made to Abraham, Isaac, and Jacob, the beloved ancestors of the people, promises that are now in jeopardy (Pr Azar 12-14), and for the sake of God's reputation among the nations, which is bound to the fortunes of the people called by God's name (vv. 11, 20-22). The author offers heartfelt sorrow and humility as a spiritual guilt offering, since the means to offer the prescribed sacrifices for sin are lacking:

> In this time we have no ruler or prophet or leader,
>> no entirely burned offering or sacrifice, no special gift or incense,
>> no place to bring gifts to you and find mercy.
> Accept us, please, with our crushed souls and humble spirits,
>> as if we brought entirely burned offerings of rams and bulls,
>> as if we brought tens of thousands of fat lambs.
> May this be the kind of offering we make in your presence today,
>> and may we follow you completely. (Pr Azar 15-17)

This prayer draws on the long-standing affirmation that the disposition of the heart of the worshiper is an essential component of any cultic offering (see, e.g., Ps 51:15-17; Mic 6:6-8). Since the latter are valueless in God's sight without the former, perhaps God will accept the former as a full substitute for the latter. This idea would become increasingly important both for Judaism and for the early church, particularly after 70 CE. It is important to note, however, that the author does not devalue the Temple cult. If it were available in these circumstances, he would offer actual animal sacrifices as the outward expression of inner sorrow for sins.

Praise

A constant movement throughout this literature is the movement from petition to praise. The dramatic action of both Tobit and Judith begins in earnest with a prayer to God for deliverance or help (Tob 3; Jdt 9) and ends with hymns celebrating God's power, goodness, and faithfulness. The Prayer of Azariah leads to the praises found in the Hymn of the Three Young Men. The authors of Prayer of Manasseh and Baruch promise public praise of God as a response to hoped-for restoration (Pr Man 15; Bar 3:6-7). Ben Sira himself offers a hymn of thanksgiving to God, who answered a prayer for deliverance that the sage had previously offered (Sir 51:1-12, esp. vv. 9-11). The counterpart to seeking God's help is giving glad testimony to the help one has experienced, and thus to the kindness and favor of the One who has brought aid. The response to receiving benefits from God is public testimony to the Benefactor, honoring God and increasing God's fame in the world (Sir 11:16-17; 12:6-7a, 20a). This is rooted in the practice of honoring and increasing the reputation of human benefactors in the ancient world.[1]

Beyond the many brief expressions of praise, for example, in the book of Tobit in response to God's deliverances throughout that tale, the Hymn of the Three Young Men (Pr Azar 28-67) provides our fullest window into new praise compositions in this period. This text is a combination of two hymns of praise composed during the intertestamental period and inserted into the narrative of Hananiah, Mishael, and Azariah in the fiery furnace as an expression of the kind of grateful response honoring God that one would expect after experiencing God's deliverance from peril.[2] Only verses 65-66 connect the hymns to this narrative context, and these could easily have been composed at the time the hymns were inserted. It is likely, then, that these hymns had a place in Jewish liturgical practice prior to this.

The first hymn addresses God directly with virtually the same phrase with which the Prayer of Azariah began:

> Blessed are you, Lord God of our ancestors.
>   You are worthy of praise and raised high above all others forever.
> (Pr Azar 29)

This echo reinforces the impression that the hymn of praise answers the petition for deliverance. The first hymn goes on to celebrate God's rule of the cosmos from his throne above the "winged creatures" (Pr Azar 31), representative of an order of angelic beings, in the heights of the heavens, his reputation that fills the world, and his presence in his temple. The second hymn takes on a different form, calling upon all the various facets of creation to give honor to their Creator:

> All works of the Lord, bless the Lord,
>   sing hymns, and lift God high above all others forever. (v. 34)

The author issues these invitations in a well-structured progression: he begins with heavenly bodies and inhabitants (vv. 35-40), then calls upon the phenomena of the realm of the sky largely associated with weather (vv. 41-50), earthly phenomena and animal inhabitants (vv. 51-58), and finally human beings in their various groupings (vv. 59-67).

The second hymn particularly shows the influence of the biblical psalms. Psalm 103:1, 20-22 features the formula "[So-and-so], bless the Lord," which opens every verse of this prayer. Psalm 148 calls upon creation in its different facets—also heavenly, meteorological, earthly, and human—to praise the Creator. Psalm 136 offers a model of a hymn with a relentless refrain in the second half of each verse, and provides, in its opening verses, the essential content of the conclusion of the Hymn of the Three. The impact of the biblical psalms on new hymns and prayers composed during this period, together with other indications of their use to give expression to prayers and praise (see, e.g., 1 Macc 4:24, which quotes Pss 118:1; 136:1), highlights the formational importance of biblical psalms for personal and corporate piety during this period.

Calendar

The practice of Judaism includes the observation of a sacred calendar, setting apart certain days as special observances related to God's dealings with the people of Israel. There is every indication that this calendar continued to play a vital role in the lives of Jews during the intertestamental period. These texts reveal a particular concern with observing the command to set the seventh day apart as a day of rest in commemoration of God's creative work, which ended in God resting, and of God's redeeming work, after which Israel, previously denied rest as slaves, could rest (Exod 20:8-11; Deut 5:12-15). So important was this command that some Jews allowed themselves to be slaughtered when attacked on the Sabbath rather than save their lives by performing what might be considered "work" and thus profaning the day (1 Macc 2:32-38). While Judas and his armies would agree to take action in self-defense, they continued to observe the Sabbath dutifully, never initiating a fight on that day (2 Macc 8:26-28; 12:38). The Sabbaths were festive occasions, not somber ones. Judith, for example, continues to fast and to wear mourning clothes years after she was widowed, but she does not fast on Sabbaths (Jdt 8:6), honoring the festivity of that holy day—as well as the festivity of days of the new moon and the regular festivals.

The celebration of these regular festivals occurs also in 1 Esdras, which attests to the ongoing observance of Passover and Booths in the postexilic period (1 Esd 5:51-52; 7:10-12). These were celebrations of God's deliverance of Israel from Egypt and provision for the people throughout their wilderness wanderings, keeping the story of Israel's foundation as a people holy for God at the forefront of their calendrical consciousness. New festivals are also instituted during this period, most notably the "Feast of Dedication" (see 1 Macc 4:56-59; John 10:22), or Hanukkah as it is now commonly known. This festival celebrated the purification of the Jerusalem Temple and its rededication to the worship of the One God after it was given over to the practice of multiple cults in the radically hellenized, multicultural Jerusalem, the first great achievement of Judas Maccabeus in 164 BCE (1 Macc 4:41-59; 2 Macc 10:1-8). Jews in Judea actively promoted the observance of this new festival, celebrating God's recent acts on behalf of God's Temple, among Jews living abroad, as the two letters now standing at the beginning of 2 Maccabees attest (1:1–2:18). There were also a number of local festivals of deliverance that appear never to have caught on, such as "Nicanor's Day" in Jerusalem (2 Macc 15:36) or the festival commemorating the rescue of Egyptian Jews from persecution (3 Macc 6:36).

In this way, the calendar of the pious Jew was punctuated with weekly, monthly, and annual reminders of the mighty acts of their God on behalf of God's people, and their identity as the distinctive people belonging to this God, and this God alone.

Temple and Liturgy

Jews of this period continued to have a deep awareness and awe for sacred space, particularly the sacred space of the Jerusalem Temple that God had chosen to be God's dwelling place on earth (Ezra 7:15; Pss 43:3; 76:2; 132:7; Tob 1:4; 2 Macc 3:38-39; 10:7; 15:34; 3 Macc 2:9), the place intimately associated with God's name and honor (Deut 12:11; 14:23, etc.; 1 Macc 7:37), the place where God's people would have special access to their God (1 Kgs 8:30; 1 Macc 7:37; 3 Macc 2:10). These people were aware that God dwelled in the heavens, even conceptualizing of the heavens as a temple where God is surrounded by angelic beings as attendants. The holy of holies in the Jerusalem Temple, however, was the space in which the two realms intersected. When the author of the Hymn of the Three Young Men writes, "Blessed are you in your glorious, holy temple, . . . Blessed are you, sitting on the winged creatures" (Pr Azar 30-31), there is no distinction between God's heavenly temple-dwelling and the holy place, between the cherubim that uphold God's throne and the mercy seat formed by the two cherubim on the lid of the ark of the covenant. Another indication of the importance of this space as the sacred space where God meets Israel is to be seen in the demonstrations around the Temple when it is threatened by foreign powers (2 Macc 3:14-22; 3 Macc 1:16-29). The mobilization of the Jerusalem population in the world of the narratives is but a reflection of the importance of this sacred space and the rites carried out therein for the religious life of the people in the world of the author and his readers. God's personal interest in this space was celebrated every year in the temple-centered Festival of Hanukkah, which told the story of God's restoration of this sacred place of meeting in response to the renewed zeal of God's people for the covenant.

The rhythms of the Temple cult affected the pulse of personal piety. Judith prays at the same time as the evening incense offering, revealing an interest in connecting prayer on the part of those removed physically from the Temple with the rhythms of Temple worship (Jdt 9:1). The channels between God and God's people were opened a little wider, the reception on both ends a little clearer, at these times of sacral activity between the two realms.

Ben Sira gives a fair amount of attention to the Temple cult in his instruction of the wise and complete Judean, nurturing an appreciation for worshiping the Lord in the beauty of holiness in the form of the liturgy of the sacrificial cult. His hymn in praise of Israel's ancestors climaxes with the description of the high priest Simon II at his priestly duties in the Temple (Sir 50:5-22). Ben Sira's description of the priest in his liturgical vestments and of the ritual itself clearly communicates the sense of awe, mystery, and wonder the sage felt as he attended these rites. His response is comparable to the awe and mystery felt during the celebration of the Mass or Eucharist for the liturgically minded Christian.

> When [Simon] put on his glorious robe
>> and clothed himself with perfect splendor,
>> when he stepped up to the holy altar,
>> he brought glory to the courts of the temple. . . .
> All Aaron's sons were in their glory,
>> and they held the Lord's offering in their hands
>> in front of the entire assembly of Israel.
> When he was finishing his service at the altar . . .
>> he poured a libation of wine . . . at the base of the altar,
>> a pleasing aroma to the Most High, the king of all.
> Then Aaron's sons cheered . . .
> [and] all the people put their faces to the ground,
>> bowing down to worship their Lord, the almighty, God Most High.
>
> The singers, accompanied by harps, sang praises with their voices;
>> they made a sweet melody with a full-bodied sound.
> The people of the Lord Most High offered prayers before the merciful one
>> until the order of the Lord's service was completed. . . .
> Then Simon came down and raised his hands
>> over the entire assembly of the Israelites
>> to give the Lord's blessing from his lips and to glorify his name.
> And they bowed down to worship a second time,
>> to receive the blessing from the Most High. (Sir 50:11, 13-21)

Many scholars have thought that Ben Sira is describing the Day of Atonement rite on account of the high priest's involvement, but it is more likely that the passage reflects the daily morning wholly burnt offering (*tamid*).[3] This daily rite involved an offering of incense (hence the priest's entrance behind, and later emergence from, the curtain; Sir 50:5), the offering of an animal, wholly consumed on the altar, and a libation offering. Ben Sira's stirring description suggests that, for like-minded worshipers, this was far from a perfunctory or empty ritual: it was a constant point of connection with the living God, to whom these offerings were made and whose blessing was imparted.

It is not surprising, therefore, that Ben Sira enthusiastically promoted the support of the Temple cult through making the regularly prescribed offerings and donations to the priests. This is so central to piety for him that he presents it as a counterpart to loving God with one's whole heart:

> Revere the Lord with your whole being,
>   and honor his priests.
> With all your might love the one who made you,
>   and don't neglect his ministers.
> Fear the Lord and honor the priest.
>   Give the priest his portion, just as you were commanded:
>   early produce, a sin offering, the gift of the shoulders, the dedicatory
>   offering, and the early produce from the holy things. (Sir 7:29-31)[4]

Participation in the Temple cult through material support of its activities is an indispensable facet of piety (see also Sir 35:6-13). Like the prophets before him, Ben Sira warns that gifts to the Temple will never convince God to wink at ill-gotten gains, as if cutting him in on a percentage (the tithe) could "buy off" the just God and make him overlook unethical practices behind the acquisition of wealth (Sir 34:21-24; 35:14-15).

Ben Sira affirms that acts of righteousness and virtue, by contrast, have value in and of themselves in God's sight, using cultic language to communicate this value:

> Whoever keeps the Law gives many offerings;
>   whoever obeys the commandments makes a sacrifice of well-being.
> Whoever repays a kindness offers the finest flour,
>   and whoever does an act of charity makes a sacrifice of praise. (Sir 35:1-4)

While Ben Sira invests such acts with the power to speak to God on behalf of the doer, as cultic acts represent communications of penitence, petition, and thanksgiving toward God, moral behavior is not a substitute for cultic involvement, any more than the latter is a substitute for the former. Ethical conduct complements, rather than replaces, participation in the Temple cult. Judith's song contains a statement minimizing the importance of the cult alongside righteous living:

> The pleasant fragrance of all offerings is a small thing to you,
>   and the fat of all entirely burned offerings means even less to you.
> But those who fear the Lord are great forever. (Jdt 16:16)

We might conclude from this that the author harbors skepticism regarding the value of the Temple sacrifices. Several psalms (e.g., Pss 40:6-8; 51:16-17) make even stronger statements in regard to the greater weight of obedience or the disposition of the heart vis-à-vis sacrificial rites, but these very psalms would have been chanted in the courts of the Temple itself. They serve rather to stress, as we have attempted to do through this and the previous chapters, that piety involved a life centered on the Torah, on the good of the neighbor, and on the rites and practices nurturing connection with God—that these were all part of a whole and that no one facet could be neglected, nor make up for deficiencies in another facet.

Chapter 6

The Jewish People and the Nations

Boundaries were very important for Jewish identity and practice. These boundaries were rooted in the very act of God's choosing one people for God's own possession from among the many peoples of the earth that God had created. The thematic commandment of Leviticus—"You must keep yourselves holy and be holy, because I [the LORD your God] am holy" (11:44; see also 11:45; 19:2)—is a call to Israel to remain distinct from other nations, to live out God's calling to *be* distinct in precisely the ways God outlined for them in the Torah. God had set them apart to stand out, in effect, and the pious Jews would indeed stand out as "different" in their neighbors' eyes. These differences led to rather sharp prejudices against Jews among non-Jews, a social reality that was particularly significant for Jews living in Diaspora in the midst of a prejudiced majority. But prejudice was not one-way. Several Jewish authors also engage in stereotyping Gentiles in unflattering ways, meeting disdain with disdain and misrepresentation with misrepresentation. The books of the Apocrypha reflect these mutual tensions and help us enter into the difficult social dynamics between Jews and Gentiles in the Second Temple period—dynamics that, frankly, have not entirely disappeared in the two intervening millennia.

Boundary Markers in Second Temple Judaism

What were the practices that set a Jew apart from the people of other nations, most clearly marking the social boundary between Jew and non-Jew? Our literature answers this question by pointing to those practices that most

95

directly occasioned prejudice and, when Judaism as a distinctive way of life was targeted for extinction in Judea under Antiochus IV, were most forcibly attacked. The writings of Greek and Latin authors, interestingly, also point to the same practices: if non-Jews knew anything about Jews, it was that they circumcised their sons, refused to perform any work every seventh day, avoided certain enjoyable foods like the plague, and denied the existence of any god but their own.

Although not typically a noticeable sign, circumcision was an extremely important and well-known marker of Jewish identity. The special covenant between the One God and the distinctive people of that God was cut into the flesh of every newborn male and the very occasional adult convert. The body of the male Jew became thereby a sign of this covenant, and thereby of the ideological boundary that existed between members of the covenant (the Jewish people) and all other peoples.[1] The author of 1 Maccabees remembers that some radical hellenizing Jews "took steps to remove the marks of circumcision" (perhaps by the procedure known as epispasm) in order to mingle more fully with the people of other races (1 Macc 1:15). This would have allowed them to appear in the public baths and to compete in athletic events as people indistinguishable from Greeks and other non-Jews, thus no longer "set apart" from other people.

Circumcision was also specifically prohibited under Antiochus IV as part of his measures to stamp out resistance to his local government in Jerusalem (i.e., the *high priest*, Menelaus!), on pain of death. This was, however, a price that several mothers were willing to pay to inscribe their sons in the covenant, showing the central importance of this identity marker (1 Macc 1:48, 60-61; 2 Macc 6:10). At the outset of their resistance activity, Mattathias and Judas targeted *un*circumcision in their attacks on disloyal Jews, forcibly circumcising Jewish boys whose parents had failed to inscribe them in the covenant (1 Macc 2:46). While we might view this as a gross violation of individual rights and personal choice in regard to religious matters, Judas and his band probably regarded it from the perspective of the collective identity (and security) of the Jewish people. It was a declaration to God and to the nation that the nation was not about to abandon the holy covenant, and that Judas and his forces would do whatever it took to maintain the nation's covenant with God.

The Jewish people followed a very different rhythm from the rest of the nations. While the latter had their own cycles of holidays and festivals, which generally meant welcome days off from work, Jews were distinctive in abstaining from all work every seventh day and in following a liturgical calendar peculiar to their people while celebrating none of the holy days of their neighbors. These practices—and avoidances of their neighbors' practices—were bound up with the Jews' commitment to One and only One God. Observing the Sabbath was a visible witness to the creative work of the One (and only) God both in fashioning the heavens and the earth (Exod 20:8-11) and in fashioning a distinctive people for himself when he brought them out from captivity in Egypt (Deut 5:12-15). The observance of the Sabbath, together with the Jews' distinctive liturgical calendar, was also proscribed under Antiochus IV. Observing the Sabbath was so important a sign of the covenant with God, and therefore a sign of the Jews' distinctive identity as God's people, that many pious Jews would not so much as use weapons to defend themselves on that day out of concern for not violating the prohibitions against work—something that their persecutors exploited to the full (1 Macc 1:43, 45; 2:29-38; 2 Macc 6:6, 11).

One of the most effective practices in terms of creating and reinforcing social boundaries, however, was the avoidance of certain foods (combined with the positive requirements that permitted foods needed to be prepared in particular ways, e.g., that animals be slaughtered by the slitting of the throat and draining of the blood). These practices virtually assured that Jews would have to create their own markets (and, therefore, their own communities to support such markets) in the cities where they lived, and that they would not go to a Gentile's home to eat food prepared by a Gentile host. Food at a Gentile's table was complicated by the fact that Gentiles "said grace" as well, honoring their gods with small offerings of wine poured out ("libations") and other acts of thanksgiving and symbols of sharing the meal not only with human guests, but with divine ones as well. Commitment to the One God and care about table fellowship and what one ate all went hand in hand. When Judith leaves the fortress town of Bethulia to enter the Assyrian camp, she takes her own food, plates, and utensils (Jdt 10:5). She does not eat the food Holofernes sets before her upon her arrival, and brings her own food and drink when dining with the general on that fateful night (12:1-4, 17-19). One of the additions to the original Hebrew version of Esther solves the problem of a Jewess living so closely with Gentiles by having Esther declare before God in prayer, "I, your servant, didn't dine at Haman's table. Nor did I honor the king's banquet or drink wine that had been offered to the gods" (Add Esth C:28).

As the author of 3 Maccabees writes about Gentile criticism and suspicion where Jews are concerned, Jewish practices of eating (and, specifically, *not* eating with their Gentile neighbors) loom large:

> While they worshipped God and conducted their lives according to God's Law, they kept themselves separate in the matter of foods. For this reason they appeared hostile to some people. But they had established a good reputation with everyone through their lifestyle of doing the right thing. Now even though the Jews' good deeds on behalf of the nation were commonly talked about by everyone, those of other races didn't take these into account. Instead, they kept harping on the differences in worship and diet, and claimed that the Jewish people were loyal neither to the king nor to the authorities, but were hostile and strongly opposed to the royal administration. And so they placed significant blame on the Jews. (3 Macc 3:4-7)

The social exclusiveness of Jews—the very thing enjoined by the Torah itself—was indeed the focal complaint of non-Jewish critics. Diodorus of Sicily, a historian from the later first century BCE, denounces the law of Moses as "an unsocial and intolerant way of life," a set of rules geared to keep Jews from pursuing normal, social interactions with people of other races (*Hist.* 34/35.1.1; 40.3.4). In the early second century CE, the Roman historian Tacitus would observe: "They sit apart at meals, and they sleep apart, and . . . they abstain from intercourse with foreign women" and men (*Hist.* 5.5).[2]

The Jewish author of the *Letter of Aristeas*, a writing from the first century BCE that attempts to explain problematic Jewish practices, would fundamentally agree with the observation of social exclusivity. He would add, however, that the Jewish Law *rightly* sets strict limits on how freely and closely Jews may mix with non-Jews:

> All human beings except [the Jews] believe in the existence of many gods, though they themselves are much more powerful than the things that they worship to no purpose. They make statues of stone and wood . . . and worship them, though they have sufficient proof to know that they have no feeling. . . . Therefore our Lawgiver, a wise person and given special endowments by God to understand all things . . . created a fence around us of impregnable barricades and iron walls, so that we might not mingle at all with people of other nations, remaining pure in body and soul, free from all false thinking, worshiping the one Almighty God above the whole creation. (*Let. Aris.* 134-35, 139)

This author understands that social boundaries are absolutely essential to preserving the Jews' distinctive commitment to monolatry in the midst of a polytheistic world. He also perceives that the dietary laws of Torah comprise a highly effective strategy for reinforcing those boundaries. It is little wonder, therefore, that Antiochus IV's representatives would use the consumption of foods forbidden by Torah as a symbol of a person's willingness (under duress) to abandon Jewish distinctiveness (1 Macc 1:63; 2 Macc 6:8, 18-20; 7:1).

Such social separatism, at the very least, violated the Greek ideal of civic unity and solidarity, and at worst aroused suspicions of antipathy against the common good. The latter connection is evident in one of the additions to Esther giving the text of the king's edict against the Jews:

> [Haman] pointed out to us that there is a certain hostile group scattered among all the peoples of the world. These people are at odds with every nation because of their peculiar laws. They constantly ignore the king's decrees, so that the government, although well managed by us, is never secure. We see that this nation stands alone in its constant hostility toward everyone. They follow a strange manner of life because of their law code, and they don't think well of our actions. They carry out the worst evils so that the kingdom is not at peace. (Add Esth B:4-5)

The same connection was evident in the passage from 3 Maccabees quoted above. Even though no specific behaviors could be cited as vicious or contrary to the common good, their exclusiveness alone was taken as evidence of hostility against non-Jews.

The ancient law that promoted such separatism, and especially those particular practices that most underscored the difference between the Jew and the non-Jew and most contributed to separate practice on the basis of distinctive identity, became the object of ridicule on the part of Gentile authors.[3] The author of 4 Maccabees places words on the lips of Antiochus IV that he might well have heard addressed to himself or a fellow Jew in conversation with a Gentile:

> You don't seem to have a mature understanding of things, since you observe the Jewish religion. Why are you disgusted by eating this animal's delicious meat? It's a gift that nature has given to us. It's stupid not to enjoy pleasant things that aren't shameful, and it's wrong to refuse nature's gifts. (4 Macc 5:7-9)

99

To the Gentile, Jewish abhorrence of pork (and the like) was incomprehensible, even an insult against Nature herself, who provided such tasty foods as a licit pleasure for human beings to enjoy.[4] The observance of the Sabbath was censured as a mark of laziness or as an excuse for cowardice (i.e., as an excuse not to go into battle).[5] The practice of circumcision was denounced as a barbaric mutilation of the body.[6] While the Greek philosopher Posidonius might admire Moses as a theologian and lawgiver, he regarded circumcision, the dietary laws, and Sabbath observance to be later creations of his followers that caused his original religion to degenerate into superstition (Strabo, *Geogr.* 16.760–61).

Jewish Criticism of Gentile Practice

If Greek and other Gentile authors trivialized and misrepresented the religion of the Jews, Jewish authors made a full return in kind. Such pillorying of the religious practices of the "other" served to underscore and reinforce the social boundaries from both sides. "They" are not like "us"; "their" foundational practices (i.e., religion) are based on fundamental error in regard to what the divine is really like and what the divine wants from human beings, unlike "our" practices; none of "us" should therefore really be enticed to become like "them" or give serious consideration to the merits of "their" way of life. Gentiles did not want their own converting to a Jewish way of life; Jews did not want their own converting (apostatizing) to a Gentile way of life. We know, however, that conversion happened, and thus that the draw both ways was quite real.

Jewish authors were particularly concerned to explain (away) or attack Gentile religious practice. People might consider converting from one religion to another, but it would be less likely if the options could be presented as "one religion" versus "no religion." The fierceness of Jewish polemics against idolatry suggests that it was not easy for Jews to hold on to their conviction that their God was the only god, and their religious devotion the only devotion of value, living in the midst of Gentiles expressing their pious and heartfelt devotion to their gods.

The Letter of Jeremiah is wholly devoted to the theme of the emptiness of Gentile religion, and is straightforward in its purpose: to insulate other Jews from the striking impression that the non-Jews' liturgies and acts of devotion could make.

In Babylon you will see gods of silver, gold, and wood paraded on the Babylonians' shoulders. These gods inspire awe among the people. Be careful that you don't become like the Gentiles, letting fear of these gods grip you, especially when you see large crowds of people walking in front of and behind them, worshipping them. But say to yourself, Lord, we want to worship you. (Let Jer 3-5)

The author directs his Jewish audience's attention away from the evidence of religious devotion in the people around them, and fixes their attention on one aspect of Gentile worship: the idols themselves. If they consider the thing itself that is worshiped, he reasons, they will be able to dismiss all the pomp and circumstance that they see in the public spaces, as well as the evident expressions of the adoration and piety felt by their neighbors.

An idol is, he argues, just a lifeless piece of metal, stone, or wood. The idol is carried around in procession because it can't even walk by itself. It gleams only if someone else polishes it. If the idol falls over, it can't stand up again on its own. If the temple catches fire, the priests may escape, but the idol will be burned up like the beams in the roof. An idol can't stop a thief from stripping off its gold and silver decorations (Let Jer 23, 25-26, 54, 57). "So why should anyone consider or call them gods?" (vv. 39, 44, 56). It is ridiculous, therefore, that anyone asks for help, or for rain, or for healing from a lifeless hunk of wood or stone. Jews, therefore, should not let the fact that women leave offerings of food and drink before the idols or that priests carry on impressively in front of them obscure the fact that a lifeless stone stands in the middle of all this to-do (vv. 29-31).

The tale of Bel and the Snake ridicules Gentile religion on similar grounds. Its author suggests that the people—including even their king—are lulled into believing that their idols are actually living gods by the trickery of their priests. The fact that the idol of Bel appears to consume each night the daily offerings of food and wine is no sign that Bel is a "living" god like the God of the Jews. Instead, there is a very rational explanation: the priests sneak in with their families each night through a secret passage and consume the offerings themselves. The cult of the idol is thus presented as the means by which clever "priests" make a living off the gullibility of the people. Actual worship of animals is rare in the ancient world, though it is attested in Egypt (where crocodiles, ibis, and falcons, for example, could be regarded as manifestations of the gods). The Jewish author again argues by reducing the practice to the absurd: Granted that an animal is living, how can it be a living *god* if it can die or be killed?

101

These texts effectively insulated other Jews from the attraction of the religious practices of their neighbors, and no doubt also effectively reinforced the social boundaries between the religiously enlightened Jew and the gullible or misguided Gentile. But they did so by means of creating a straw person argument. Gentiles did not understand themselves to be worshiping the statues in their temples or the sacred animals in and of themselves: they understood the statue or the animal to be a physical representation of the divinity with whom they sought to interact, whose being was by no means limited by these representations.[7] Thus the lifelessness of the idol was merely a quality of the representation, not a quality of the god represented, who was ever so much more and so far beyond the idol. More philosophically minded Greek and Roman authors would concur with the Jewish critique of using idols, while nevertheless holding on to the reality of their own gods. For example, Varro, the first-century BCE Roman philosopher, approved of the fact that Jews rejected giving their God any physical representation and criticized his own people for abandoning the original, pure, Roman practice of not representing deity in physical form (quoted in Augustine, *Civ.* 4.31).

Wisdom of Solomon 13:1–15:17 presents a somewhat more sophisticated critique of Gentile religion. While this author also uses the reductionistic arguments already encountered (13:10-19), he shows some understanding that more stands behind the practice of idolatry than the worship of sticks and stones as he theorizes about the origin of idolatrous cults. He imagines a father mourning the loss of his child. He makes an image of the child in order to hold on to her, and treats the statue as if it were alive. After the practice continues, he gives orders to the people under his authority to do the same and to continue to honor the statue with special ceremonies after his own death. This continues for generations, with people forgetting the very human origins of the cult, and an idolatrous cult is born (Wis 14:15-16).[8] He is thus able to explain the practice of idolatry for his Jewish audience, while at the same time undermining any value in the practice.

Nevertheless, despite this greater sophistication, the author's polemic is still geared toward arousing prejudice and contempt for non-Jews on account of their religious practices. Gentiles "who don't know God are empty-headed by nature" (Wis 13:1). They recognized the beauty of creation in their worship of the stars of heaven, but failed to deduce the existence and nature of the Creator from the order and beauty of God's handiwork (13:1, 5-9). Gentiles cannot be virtuous people: their perverted ideas about the divine lead systematically to the perversion of their social order, their relationships, their very being and drives:

> The worship of nameless idols is the origin of all evil—its cause as well as its result. People begin to party so wildly that they all go mad. They prophesy lies. They live in such a way that everything they do is wrong. They bear false witness, but because they have entrusted themselves into the hands of lifeless idols, they don't expect any harm to come from swearing false pledges. (Wis 14:27-29)

Gentile idolaters can't be trusted to return favors, respect other people's marriages, or recognize virtue. Differences in religious belief and practice lead to the conclusion that Gentiles are thoroughly depraved: their minds are alienated from the truth, and their lifestyle is "vile and depraved" (3 Macc 4:16; 6:9). The intensity and frequency of such rhetoric suggest that, indeed, Diaspora Jews "needed the passions of contempt and hatred for the religion of their neighbors to protect their faith from the daily allure of paganism," and from neighbors who would have welcomed them into their temples (Bickerman 1988, 256).

Openness to Gentile Ideas

At the same time, the books of the Apocrypha also show that Jews exhibited a significant degree of openness to foreign wisdom and intellectual resources, even while, for the most part, maintaining high social boundaries and a dismissal of the value of the Gentiles in God's sight en masse. Ben Sira, the Jerusalem sage and teacher, wrote that it was part of the scribe's duty to "travel in foreign lands" in order to "test what's good and what's evil in people" (Sir 39:4), gathering what is valuable from the wisdom of other nations for incorporation into his own teaching. Ben Sira himself appears to have learned and incorporated into his own curriculum much from the instruction found in the *Elegies* of the sixth-century BCE Greek sage Theognis concerning caution about the company one keeps, choosing confidants, the value of old friends over more recent ones, the importance of patience when friends wrong you, caution regarding slandering a friend or believing a damaging report about a friend, and care in choosing whom one will benefit. Similarly, the correspondences between Ben Sira and the Egyptian *Instruction of Phibis* on the topics of being cautious in dealing with the powerful, in choosing one's friends, against slander, and in showing proper social etiquette further reflect the Jerusalem sage's regard for the wisdom of other nations.[9]

The author of the Wisdom of Solomon promotes the pursuit of the Wisdom given by God (exhibited in the person whose life is aligned with God's Law) on the basis of its training a person in the cardinal virtues prized by Platonists and Stoics—justice, courage, temperance, and prudence (Wis 8:7). The author's view of the human being as a soul once existing prior to and apart from a human body (8:19-20), for a time being burdened by a body (an "earthly container" weighing down the mind; 9:15), and then being released again for immortality, is a view adopted from Greek psychology.[10]

Perhaps most notable for his adoption of Greek philosophical ideals, language, and goals is the author of 4 Maccabees. He accepts, as a worthy goal for the Jew, the Greek ethical ideal of the mastery of the passions that get in the way of choosing the virtuous course of action, and shows close interaction with Gentile philosophers' discussion of that subject, as well as the topics of fraternal affection and love for offspring (sharing many details with Aristotle's and Plutarch's treatments of these subjects). He uses this information to interpret the Torah-centered life as the God-given training program by means of which any individual, of any temperament, can gain mastery over desires, emotions, and sensations and be thus equipped to choose the path of virtue in any situation, no matter how difficult.

But while these authors show an eager willingness to use Pharaoh's gold, as it were, they do not evince a great openness to Pharaoh.

Gentiles in the People and Plan of God?

Another indicator of the tensions that existed between Jews and people of other races during this period is the relatively low expectation that the authors of the books of the Apocrypha have in regard to Gentile conversion to the worship of the One God—as well as the correspondingly low openness to Gentiles joining the people of God or even falling within the purview of God's plan for God's future kingdom.

First Esdras, like the closely related texts Ezra and Nehemiah, defines the boundaries of Israel very narrowly on the basis of legitimate bloodlines. So sharp are these boundaries that the foreign wives of those Jews who returned from exile are not given the option of converting to Judaism. Rather, they must simply be divorced and the children of mixed marriages disavowed.

The author of Wisdom of Solomon appears to take a more open view of non-Jews as he considers God's dealings with people of other races. He affirms of God in prayer, "You love everything that exists. You despise nothing that you have made" (Wis 11:24). Because of this, God did not destroy the Canaanites all at once, but rather judged them "little by little to give them an opportunity to change their hearts and minds" (12:10a). This represents a striking development of Exodus 23:29-30: there, God's rationale for driving out the Canaanites only little by little was to keep the promised land from becoming desolate and overrun with wild animals. Here, the rationale is grounded in God's justice and God's mercy toward sinful (and non-Jewish) people. Wisdom of Solomon also represents a step forward from the position of 2 Maccabees, whose author affirms that God judges God's people Israel immediately when they begin to turn astray, so as to discipline them and get them back on a healthful track, but "with other nations the Lord patiently delays punishment until they fill up the full measure of their sins," intervening for their destruction rather than their correction (2 Macc 6:13-16).

Despite this, the author of Wisdom does not nurture high hopes of Gentiles' changing their hearts and minds. God disciplined the Canaanites little by little "even though [God] knew full well that they were wicked from their birth, that their natural inclination was to evil, and that they would never change their minds" (Wis 12:10b). Similarly, none of God's warnings were effective for moving the Egyptians to repentance. Rather, "a fate they fully deserved drew them to this inevitable decision and made them forget about all the things that had so recently happened to them" (19:4), namely the warnings of the ten plagues. God's forbearance toward Gentile nations, in the end, says more about God's patient and merciful character than about any real hope for the non-Jewish peoples.

It is only in the story of Judith that we find a portrait of a full convert to Judaism in the person of Achior the Ammonite. He is a Gentile who understands the covenant relationship between God and God's people Israel (Jdt 5:5-21). His confession of this knowledge joins him in a preliminary way to the people of Bethulia as he is sent there by Holofernes to share their fate (6:2-13). After witnessing the power of God to deliver God's people, he joins them, notably accepting circumcision as a sign that he had crossed over the boundary into the people of God (14:10).

Despite the Jewish people's confession that their God created and gave life to all people, the authors of the Apocrypha fairly consistently conceive of God as concerned only with the well-being of his chosen people, and as taking their side in their conflicts with people of other races rather than standing by impartially. The two additions to Esther that, in the Greek version, frame the whole narrative present the non-Jewish nations standing at variance against the Jewish nation—notably, the "righteous nation" (Add Esth F:5). The only meaningful categories in God's sight, according to this author, would be "Jew" and "non-Jew." The Festival of Purim ("lots") is itself given a new layer of interpretation, for now there is one "lot" for the Jewish people and one common "lot" for all the rest of the nations, and God aligns God's own interests clearly with the first, "*his* people" and "*his* inheritance" (Add Esth F:7-9).

The author of 3 Maccabees expresses a very similar view. He affirms that God cares for God's people Israel, "even when they were in the land of their enemies" (3 Macc 6:15, quoting Lev 26:44). He gives no expression of hope, however, for the conversion and inclusion of the people of other races. He hopes only that such people will become witnesses to God's special care for the Jewish people. After a preliminary sign of rescue, the Jews rounded up in the hippodrome pray that God "would show the might of his exceedingly strong hand to the arrogant Gentiles" (5:13). At the climactic moment, Eleazar prays in the midst of the hippodrome, "Let it be shown to all the Gentiles that you are with *us*, Lord" (6:15, emphasis added). After God's deliverance of God's people, King Ptolemy confesses that "the heavenly God surely shields the Jews and fights alongside them as a father for his children" (7:6). At no point does this God also become Ptolemy's God, nor is any hope kindled that God will gather Jews and Gentiles together as one people in the worship of the One God.

Perhaps the most radical expression of a presumption of God's partiality toward God's historic people Israel is to be found in the apocalypse known as 4 Ezra (2 Esd 3–14), written a few decades after the Roman armies suppressed the Jewish Revolt and destroyed Jerusalem and its Temple:

> "You have said that the other nations born of Adam are nothing, that they are like spit, and you have compared their abundance to a drop from a pitcher. But look now, Lord! These nations that are valued as nothing rule over us and devour us, while we, your people, whom you have called your oldest offspring, your one and only child, those who are zealous for you, your dearest ones, are handed over to them. If the world was created for our sake, why don't we possess our world as an inheritance? How long will this situation last?" (2 Esd 6:56-59)

The author refers to a passage in Isaiah 40:15-17, where the point of diminishing "all the nations" (v. 17) is to emphasize the limitless greatness and power of God. This author, however, reads the passage as an absolute statement about God's lack of regard for the non-Jewish peoples, adding the colorful image of "spit" to express this lack of worth. The presenting problem, of course, is Rome's continued vigor and prosperity (not to mention domination of Israel) after its actions against God's Holy City and Temple. Granted that Israel may have had it coming on account of its transgressions, shouldn't Rome be suffering an even worse fate right about now? As this author looks ahead, he does see God acting on behalf of Israel, bringing judgment against Rome, but he extends no hope for the inclusion of Gentiles in the worshiping people of God.

The author of 4 Ezra also pushes beyond a simple theology of election, according to which belonging to Israel is in itself sufficient for deliverance (whether in this world or for the next), to an insistence on committed observance of the covenant as the prerequisite to being part of the people God has chosen for eternity (see 2 Esd 7:52-58, 127-129). However, he does not take the step of suggesting that doing what pleases God is alone sufficient for enjoying the fruits of election. Descent from Israel may not be sufficient, but it remains, nevertheless, indispensable.

It is difficult not to read such texts without hearing Paul's burning question: "Is God the God of Jews only? Isn't God the God of Gentiles also?" (Rom 3:29). Nevertheless, if we understand the nature and degree of the social tension between Jews and Gentiles both in the land of Israel (e.g., in the wake of the repression of Judaism under Antiochus IV or of the Roman destruction and occupation of Jerusalem) and throughout the Diaspora, we can understand how, for the most part, it was difficult for a pious Jew to look beyond the need for God's vindication of the Jew's trust in that God in the face of his or her neighbors' contempt and, sometimes, hostility.

The book of Baruch also gives expression to hopes for God's future interventions in the world on behalf of God's chastened people (Bar 4:30–5:9). The author promises that the cities of Jerusalem's enemies, who have mistreated her and who have received her exiled children, will themselves come to misery. God will "strip away the pride" of the capital city of the empire God has used to punish Jerusalem for the people's violations of the covenant "and turn her arrogance into grief. The eternal one will send fire on her for many days, and demons will inhabit her for a long time" (4:34-35). Jerusalem will again receive her exiled sons and daughters, who will be "gathered from the west to the east" (5:5). This, however, is as far as the author will see. There is no conversion of the nations, or inclusion of the same in the worship of the One God—only their punishment.

Among these texts, Tobit—and Tobit only—preserves a strikingly inclusive vision of the future that God will bring about. In addition to rhapsodizing on the future gathering of God's dispersed people Israel into their ancestral land, the author holds out hope for the conversion of the nations to faith in the One God:

> A bright light will shine forth into the farthest corners of the earth.
> Many nations will come to you from afar,
> and inhabitants from all the ends of the earth will come to your
> holy name.
> They will bear gifts in their hands for the king of heaven. (Tob 13:11)

After the end-time gathering in of the exiles and rebuilding of the Temple in splendor (not as it was rebuilt upon the first return of exiles from Babylon), "all the nations of the whole earth will turn and genuinely revere God. They will all leave behind their idols that have deceived them and led them into error. They will praise the eternal God in righteousness" (Tob 14:6-7). Tobit is most fully aligned with the vision of the Hebrew prophets concerning the future conversion of the nations, a vision that Jesus appears to have upheld when he insisted that his fellow Jews continue to keep the Gentiles' place in the Temple sacrosanct for God's future purposes for them (Mark 11:17, reciting Isa 56:7-8).

Tensions Among Jews

Concern over the boundaries between Jews and the people of other nations did not come to expression only in interracial tensions. Tensions within the Jewish community over such matters were just as palpable, if not more virulent. Even more corrosive of Jewish commitment and identity than Gentile misunderstanding and ridicule was the informed defection of Jews from their ancestral way of life. Whether such abandonment of the distinctive practices marking Jews as a people set apart arose from a person's or family's desire to avoid harassment or to gain positive advantages through assimilation, apostasy aroused stronger reactions from Jews than Gentile prejudice ever did.

The author of 3 Maccabees paints a scenario in which considerable political pressure was being applied to the Jewish community in Egypt to leave behind their distinctive way of life, participate in the city's cults, and receive the gift of citizenship in Alexandria:

> Some Jews, while pretending to detest the steps to be undertaken for the city's religion, readily surrendered themselves to share in great fame through the association they would have with the king. But the honorable majority were strong and didn't depart from their religion. They bravely tried to save themselves from being registered by resorting to bribes in exchange for their lives. They remained hopeful of obtaining help, and they looked with contempt on those Jews who had deserted them. They considered those who gave in to be enemies of the Jewish nation, and no longer associated with them or offered them assistance. (3 Macc 2:31-33)

The Jews who remained loyal to their way of life could use shunning and other shaming techniques as a means of trying to pressure the apostate Jews into returning to a Torah-observant way of life. At the very least, such social manifestations of disapproval would warn those considering adapting too far to the Greek way of life that they would need to make a definitive choice between the two worlds rather than hope to straddle them.

The intensity of this inner-Jewish pressure emerges more sharply at the end of this piece of historical fiction. After the faithful Jews' deliverance,

> they petitioned the king that they might carry out the punishment deserved by those Jews who had voluntarily turned aside from the holy God and God's Law. They insisted that those who had broken divine laws for the sake of the belly would never be reliable subjects under the king's government either. The king recognized and agreed that they were speaking the truth. So he gave them a free hand to utterly destroy those who had violated God's Law in every place within his kingdom. . . . They punished and killed any fellow Jews they came upon who had polluted themselves, making a public example of them. On that day they killed more than three hundred persons, a day that they also observed as a joyous festival since they had subdued the renegades. (3 Macc 7:10-12, 14-15)

What is striking in this fantasy of the violent elimination of apostate Jews is that the renegade Jews are treated, in effect, as the real enemy, and not Ptolemy and his enforcers (the most obvious antagonists in the plot of 3 Maccabees).

A somewhat inverted portrait of the relationship between both Torah-observant and apostate Jews emerges in the opening chapters of the Wisdom of Solomon, where the author describes the antagonism of the wicked against the righteous person (Wis 1:16–2:24). The author's description of the wicked suggests that they are not Gentiles, but Jews. They decide to take action against the righteous person because "he blames us because we have failed to keep the Law" and "condemns us for turning our backs on our upbringing" (2:12). The implication is that they are themselves Jews who have left the Torah-observant life behind. Their actions against the righteous Jew—degrading and torturing him to death!—are meant to prove that his claims about the value of Torah observance (and, therefore, his claims about the fundamental errors of their own choices) are false. His bad end will prove the emptiness of his hope.

These dynamics of extreme mutual animosity require some explanation. To the Jew who remains loyal to the Torah, the apostate Jew represents, in the first instance, a threat to the whole nation. According to Deuteronomy 27–32, God's preservation and protection of the Jewish people as a whole are linked to the people's obedience as a whole. One does not know in advance where the "tipping point" is, but every apostate (who, thereby, flagrantly disregards Torah) advances the nation toward that tipping point. Attempting to correct the apostate—or in the worst-case scenario, to destroy the apostate—is a pursuit closely bound up with the preservation of the nation's covenant with the One God. But the apostate is a threat to the individual as well. Gentiles have historically never understood the value of the covenant or the God with whom the covenant puts one in relationship. An apostate, however, knowingly turns away from the same as something of less value than fuller acceptance by, and advancement within, non-Jewish society. The apostate (or simply the Jew who relaxes the boundaries) is a witness that any rewards of Torah observance in all its particulars are not worth their price. Conversely, for the apostate Jew, the Jew who perseveres in Torah observance is a constant reminder of the way of life, the social networks, and the social identity one has left behind. The ongoing life of the Torah-observant Jewish community has the potential of raising grave doubts in the apostate's mind concerning the wisdom of his or her choices—and, no doubt, the Torah-observant Jews are not silent on this point either. The resulting mutual antagonism and rejection are mechanisms by which to affirm the social identity one has chosen, and the antagonism is sharper because the threat to that identity comes now from within the community itself.

One other important strained intra-Jewish dynamic is reflected in the Apocrypha and needs to be mentioned: the relationship between the residents of Samaria and its environs and the Judean people. The former regarded themselves as the remnants of the northern tribes of Israel. Like their neighbors to the south, they regulated their lives by the law of Moses (specifically, the "five books of Moses") and faithfully worshiped the God of Israel, though they did so at a temple beside Mount Gerizim, newly built in the years after Alexander the Great's seizure of the region. The Judeans, on the other hand, questioned the Samaritans' genealogical integrity as descendants of the northern tribes, regarding the Samaritans instead as a people of mixed blood and their religion as a mixture of Jewish and pagan rites (see the story of their origins in 2 Kgs 17:24-31). When the Samaritans offered to help rebuild the Jerusalem Temple in the Persian period (Ezra 4:1-5), the returning Judeans rejected their partnership in a decisive rejection of any kinship with them. The ongoing hostility between these people groups continues through the Hellenistic period and is reflected in Ben Sira's passing, derisive comments:

> My spirit takes offense at two nations,
>   and the third is not even a nation:
>   those who settled on Samaria's hills [Hebrew, "in Edom"],
>   the Philistines,
>   and the foolish people who dwell in Shechem. (Sir 50:25-26)

The nadir of Judean-Samaritan relations would come in the Hasmonean period, when John Hyrcanus I destroyed Samaria, Shechem, and the Samaritan temple (see Josephus, *Ant.* 13.9.1 §§254–256; 13.10.2–3 §§275–283).

The Apocrypha and the Social World of the Early Church

These texts, and the social dynamics they reflect, are essential background to understanding the social world of the New Testament. Only when we understand the importance for most Jews of the boundary markers between Jew and Gentile that Paul treats so lightly will we adequately understand and sympathetically view Jewish (and some Jewish-Christian) resistance to Paul's mission to bring together Jews and Gentiles in the "one body" of the church on equal terms. The inner-Jewish social dynamics of pressuring renegades to return to more fully covenant-observant practices are at work in Paul's own pre-Christian persecution of Jesus' followers (Acts 8:2-3; 9:1-2; Gal 1:13), in the mission of the so-called Judaizers to bring Gentile Christians within the boundaries of Judaism through circumcision and adoption of a Torah-observant lifestyle (Acts 15:1; Gal 5:2-7, 12; 6:12-13), and in the hostile reactions to Paul's work in city after city (Acts 13:44-47, 50; 14:2, 19; Gal 5:11; 1 Thess 2:14b-16; etc.).

We also begin to understand how radical and unsettling Paul's proclamations concerning the boundary-marking practices of the Jewish people were:

> Being circumcised or not being circumcised doesn't matter in Christ Jesus, but faith working through love does matter. (Gal 5:6)

> One person considers some days to be more sacred than others, while another person considers all days to be the same. Each person must have their own convictions. (Rom 14:5)

> I know and I'm convinced in the Lord Jesus that nothing is wrong to eat in itself. But if someone thinks something is wrong to eat, it becomes wrong for that person. (Rom 14:14; see also 1 Tim 4:3-5)

Paul was engaged in a radical redefinition of what was required to belong to the people of God, a redefinition that struck at the core of Jewish self-understanding as the people of God based on careful observance of those practices that set them apart from Gentiles.

Moreover, as the Christian movement develops, it inherits and uses increasingly the apologetic and polemical strategies employed by both Jews against Gentile practice and by Gentiles against Jewish practice as it forms its own identity as something of a third entity accepted by neither non-Christian Jews nor Gentiles. Entering more fully into these social dynamics also helps us appreciate the achievement of the Christian movement where it was able to bring Jews and non-Jews together into one body against the force of centuries of prejudice and mutual antagonism. It also helps explain some of the failures and fractures within the early Christian movement, as Gnostics succumb to the historic Gentile prejudice against the Jewish revelation (i.e., against the Hebrew Bible and "its" God) and as Jewish-Christian groups succumb to the historic Jewish insistence on the priority of becoming part of the distinctive, Jewish people to experience the deliverance of Israel's Messiah.

Chapter 7

The Apocrypha and the Christian Church

The church of the second century and beyond drew inspiration and sought guidance from the books of the Apocrypha alongside the books of the Old and the New Testaments. Many church fathers make explicit reference to the books of Wisdom, Ben Sira, Baruch, and others, reciting passages from the same as valuable, even authoritative, texts relevant to the issues at hand in the early church. On the basis of such explicit use, we can readily see the influence of these texts on the emerging church in its most formative centuries.

New Testament authors, most if not all of whom wrote before 100 CE, never make such explicit references, nor do they ever actually quote a passage from any apocryphal book. Even in the earliest generation of the church, however, one can readily discern the impact of the teaching and stories found in the Apocrypha. Even while they do not recite passages verbatim, the authors of the New Testament frequently show that they have been informed by these texts, have approved what they have learned, and have incorporated this into their own message.

In the absence of explicit citation, demonstrating influence does require more care. It involves more than finding parallels in thought and content. We need to be able to show that the "influencing" text was available to the person or text being influenced, and well positioned to enter into the streams of tradition from which the later author or speaker drank. The content also needs to be sufficiently distinctive to both texts such that other explanations (e.g., common dependence on an even older, shared tradition) are excluded.

113

Similarity in wording and expression can function as supporting evidence, as well as pervasiveness of influence. That is to say, if there are many parallels between the "influencing" text and "influenced" material, and if these parallels occur from various parts of the former on various parts of the latter, the case for influence becomes even stronger.

The fact that the earliest Christians do not explicitly cite these books probably has bearing on the authority generally accorded these books in the circles to whom they were writing and within which they lived. Given the fact that most of the earliest Christian leaders were Jewish, and the fact that the books of the Apocrypha never gained canonical authority in the synagogue, it should not surprise us that the New Testament authors do not treat these texts as they do the commonly agreed-upon Scriptures—those books whose unquestioned authority made it profitable for one's own case to cite them in support. Given the utter neglect into which these books have fallen in many modern Christian circles, however, it should greatly surprise us to discover how much leaders like Paul, James, the author of Hebrews, and Jesus himself appear to have learned, valued, and incorporated from the texts later labeled "Apocrypha."

Ben Sira, Jesus, and James

In the Gospel according to Matthew, Jesus' teaching ministry begins in earnest with a collection of instructions known as the "Sermon on the Mount." The first third of this sermon is dominated by a pattern in which Jesus quotes what "was said to those who lived long ago" as a means of introducing what Jesus would himself say to those present before him (Matt 5:21, 27, 31, 33, 38, 43). It is common to read this as a sign that what Jesus teaches is different from and *opposed to* what had been taught in the Torah or in earlier sages' instruction, but in fact what Jesus goes on to teach in this sermon represents rather a tightening of the Torah and includes many principles and promotes many practices that Jesus had received from earlier sages like Ben Sira. Jesus was certainly an innovative teacher, but much more of his teaching has a "pedigree" than is often supposed.[1]

For example, Jesus teaches that forgiving fellow human beings is prerequisite to seeking forgiveness for the sins one has committed against God oneself. This teaching is embedded in the brief prayer that Jesus taught his disciples:

Forgive us for the ways we have wronged you,
just as we also forgive those who have wronged us. (Matt 6:12)

Forgive us our sins,
for we also forgive everyone who has wronged us. (Luke 11:4)

This is the only petition that received specific comment in Matthew's arrangement of the Sermon on the Mount. At the conclusion of the prayer, Jesus explains: "If you forgive others their sins, your heavenly Father will also forgive you. But if you don't forgive others, neither will your Father forgive your sins" (Matt 6:14-15; cf. Mark 11:25). One of Jesus' parables—the parable of the unforgiving servant (Matt 18:23-35)—underscores the connection between being forgiven our offenses against God and forgiving those who have offended us.

Although Jesus emphasizes this teaching, and although we do not find this teaching in the Hebrew Bible, it did not originate with him. Two centuries before his birth, Ben Sira had taught that anyone who hopes to be forgiven by God must not harbor unforgiveness toward fellow mortals:

Forgive your neighbor a wrong,
and then, when you pray, your sins will be forgiven.
Can people hold on to their anger against others,
and then look for healing from the Lord?
Can they refuse to have mercy on people like themselves,
and then pray about their own sins?
If they, who are just flesh, hold on to anger,
who will secure pardon for their own sins? (Sir 28:2-5)

God's honor is incomparably greater than the honor of any human being. If humans expect God to forgive offenses against God's self rather than avenge the slight to his honor that disobedience represents, they must not presume to cherish grudges. To do so, while expecting God to forgive slights, would be to treat one's own honor as greater than God's. Therefore, such people "will suffer the Lord's vengeance" (Sir 28:1), a consequence that Jesus dramatically displays in his parable of the unforgiving servant. As the king handed the unforgiving servant over to be tortured perpetually, "my heavenly Father will also do the same to you if you don't forgive your brother or sister from your heart" (Matt 18:35).

Jesus is remembered to have invited people to learn from him the way of life that pleases God and leads to success with these winsome words: "Come to me, all you who are struggling hard and carrying heavy loads, and I will give you rest. Put on my yoke, and learn from me. I'm gentle and humble. And you will find rest for yourselves. My yoke is easy to bear, and my burden is light" (Matt 11:28-30).

The invitation to "come" to approach a teacher and to "take up" a "yoke" of instruction, accompanied by the promise that, by so doing, one would find "rest" without the journey becoming burdensome, brings together elements and forms familiar from Ben Sira's invitation to the elite youth of Jerusalem more than two centuries before:

> Draw near to me,
> you who lack education,
>   and stay in my school. . . .
> I opened my mouth and said,
> "Acquire [Wisdom] for yourselves without money.
>
> Place your neck under her yoke,
> and let your soul receive instruction.
> It is found close at hand."
>
> See for yourselves that I have labored a little,
>   and I have found much rest for myself. (Sir 51:23, 25-27)

By issuing such an invitation, employing the familiar imagery of taking on a particular yoke and laboring (but little) to find rest, and by frequently using the forms of maxims, sayings, and instructions in his teaching, Jesus appears to have presented himself in the role of a wisdom teacher or sage, one who showed the way to live in a manner well pleasing to God and advantageously among people, giving his contemporaries an important and recognizable category (by no means the *only* one, of course) for understanding his ministry and purpose.

While promoting charitable aid is fully in keeping with the Torah and the prophetic literature, Jesus introduces several topics and images that cannot be derived from the Hebrew Bible, but do appear in Ben Sira's exhortations to charity, in the course of his own extensive exhortations to generosity toward those in need. Jesus urges his followers, "Give to those who ask, and don't refuse those who wish to borrow from you" (Matt 5:42). Jesus promotes this behavior by claiming that those who thus mirror the generosity of God show themselves to be "children of your Father who is in heaven" (5:45). Ben Sira had similarly exhorted his pupils to care for the poor, and regarded this as the means by which they, too, would show themselves to be children of the God whose own character it was to care for the marginal and needy:

> Don't keep rejecting the plea of someone in distress,
>   and don't turn your face away from the poor.
> Don't turn your eyes away from someone begging,
>   and don't give anyone an opportunity to curse you. . . .
> Be like a parent to orphans,
>   and take care of their mothers as [you would] your own wife or husband.
>   Do this, and you will be like a child of the Most High,
>   and God will love you more than your own mother does. (Sir 4:4-5, 10)

Ben Sira, however, instructed his students to limit their charity and generosity to people of proven character, people who had shown themselves pious by living in alignment with the Torah:

> If you do good,
> know for whom you do it,
>   and there'll be gratitude for your good deeds. . . .
> Give to the pious, but don't assist sinners.
> Do good to the humble,
> but don't give to the ungodly.
>   Hold back your bread, and don't give it to them,
>   since by it they might gain power over you. . . .
> Give to good people,
> and don't assist sinners. (Sir 12:1, 4-5, 7)[2]

Ben Sira sets these limits based on his understanding of the limits of God's own generosity: "The Most High also hated sinners, and he will repay the ungodly with punishment" (Sir 12:6). Jesus, however, acknowledges no such limits. Rather, Jesus urges giving to those in need irrespective of the merits of the recipient in imitation of the God who sends the gifts of sun and rain "on both the righteous and the unrighteous" alike, out of God's perfect generosity (Matt 5:45). Nevertheless, the roots of Jesus' teaching that a person reflects kinship with God to the extent that he or she shares God's generous character are otherwise present in Ben Sira.

117

Ben Sira also promoted giving away money to the needy as, somewhat ironically, the means by which to "lay up a treasure" for oneself, the kind of treasure that would become one's best defense against unforeseen future need:

> Help the needy for the commandment's sake,
>   and in proportion to their need
>   don't turn them away empty-handed.
> Part with silver for a relative's or friend's sake,
>   and don't let it corrode under a stone and be destroyed.
> Invest your treasure according to the commandments of the Most High,
>   and it will profit you more than gold.
> Store up acts of charity in your treasuries,
>   and it will deliver you from every distress. (Sir 29:9-12)[3]

Jesus would later use this contrast between the typical way a person stored up wealth as a provision for his or her future needs (i.e., stockpiling material wealth) and the way to store up a treasure in God's economy (i.e., by giving away what one does not need for today to those presently in need):

> "Stop collecting treasures for your own benefit on earth, where moth and rust eat them and where thieves break in and steal them. Instead, collect treasures for yourselves in heaven, where moth and rust don't eat them and where thieves don't break in and steal them." (Matt 6:19-20)

> Sell your possessions and give to those in need. Make for yourselves wallets that don't wear out—a treasure in heaven that never runs out. No thief comes near there, and no moth destroys. (Luke 12:33; see also Matt 19:21)

Like Ben Sira, Jesus asserts that the stash of money that sits idle rather than being spent in works of mercy ends up being lost to corrosion and theft. Unlike Ben Sira, however, who understands the treasure laid up through generosity as a source of help against future times of adversity in this life, Jesus regards this treasure as one's wealth in God's sight, which will be manifested in heaven. Nevertheless, Jesus appears to have incorporated into his own teaching Ben Sira's principle that one really "keeps" only what one gives away to help those in greater need, and that one's best investment is to relieve a needy person's present necessity.[4]

This is not to say that Jesus would have agreed with everything taught by the older Jerusalem sage. Jesus' attitude toward women, for example, reveals a point of sharp disagreement. Ben Sira writes some bitter words about women (see esp. Sir 7:20-26; 9:1-9; 23:16-27; 25:13–26:27; 36:26-31; 40:19b; 42:9-14). He complains that "a daughter's birth is a liability" (22:3) and asserts that "a man's wickedness is better than a woman who does good" (42:14). Ben Sira reflects the expectations, values, and anxieties of his society. A man's honor was at stake if his wife or daughter were sexually compromised by another man (42:11). Ben Sira's contempt for women is ultimately a product—and projection—of his culture's obsession with female sexuality as a point of vulnerability for a male's honor. [5]

Jesus did not share Ben Sira's point of view. While Ben Sira would relegate women to the inner spaces of the house where other men would have no access to them, Jesus invited women into the male spaces of the home, the city, and the countryside where disciples gathered to learn from Jesus (see Luke 8:1-3; 10:38-42). He valued women as disciples and witnesses, regarding them as persons worthy of dialogue and instruction, not reducing their moral worth to the spheres of their silence, submissiveness, or sexuality.

Ben Sira appears to have informed the wisdom of another, later Jewish sage who took up residence in Jerusalem, namely James, the half brother of Jesus. Because human speech is so problematic, it is not surprising to find many ancient sages reflecting on its dangers and giving counsel concerning guarding one's speech. This topic is prominent in both Ben Sira's wisdom and James's circular letter to Jewish followers of Jesus. Ben Sira regarded speech (referred to by the name of the body part presumed to produce speech, namely the tongue) as a source of great danger to oneself and to others. The tongue required constant vigilance, but, for all one's watchfulness, poison darts still slipped by:

> Who will put a guard on my mouth
>   and an effective seal upon my lips
> so that I don't fall
> because of my speech
> and so that my tongue
> doesn't destroy me? (Sir 22:27)

> Who hasn't sinned with the tongue? (Sir 19:16)

> [The tongue] will never conquer the godly,
>   and they won't be burned by its flame.
> Those who abandon the Lord will fall to it;
>   it will burn within them,
>   and it will never go out. (Sir 28:22-23)

When James speaks of the dangers of malicious speech or ill-spoken words, he picks up on the striking metaphor of a "fire" that sets all that surrounds it ablaze to depict the inflammatory power of speech, also admitting that the tongue's unruliness is beyond human power to tame completely:

> The tongue is a small flame of fire, a world of evil at work in us. It contaminates our entire lives. Because of it, the circle of life is set on fire. The tongue itself is set on fire by the flames of hell. . . . No one can tame the tongue, though. It is a restless evil, full of deadly poison. (Jas 3:6, 8)

The fact that speech could at one time be sweet and healing and at another time be bitter and wounding made it, in effect, an anomaly within the natural order. Ben Sira expressed wonder that such opposites could come from the same source, namely the mouth: "If you blow on a spark, it will flame up, and if you spit on it, it will go out; nonetheless, both come out of your mouth" (Sir 28:12). He went on, then, to talk about the harm caused by slanderous speech, urging that people keep very close guard over what they say so as to prevent the harmful effects of hurtful words (28:13-26). James also reflects on the tongue as a creature that stands out and apart from the rest of nature because of its ability to put forth such different fruit:

> With it we both bless the Lord and Father and curse human beings made in God's likeness. Blessing and cursing come from the same mouth. My brothers and sisters, it just shouldn't be this way!
> Both fresh water and salt water don't come from the same spring, do they? My brothers and sisters, can a fig tree produce olives? Can a grapevine produce figs? Of course not, and fresh water doesn't flow from a saltwater spring either. (Jas 3:9-12)

Speaking both for blessing and for cursing is, therefore, wholly unnatural, and the wise must bring greater integrity to their lives and convictions by reserving the use of their tongues for bringing blessing both to God and to human beings created in God's image.

The two sages also both address the theological problem of the source of temptation in a world ruled by an omnipotent and righteous God, and thus the question of who is ultimately responsible for sin. Both sages assert that the problem cannot be resolved by laying this responsibility upon God:

> Don't say, "I fell away because of the Lord."
> What the Lord hates, he won't do.

Don't say, "The Lord made me go astray."
　He has no use for sinful people.
The Lord has hated every foul thing,
　and those who fear him have no love for such things. . . .
He doesn't command anyone to be ungodly,
　and he doesn't give anyone a license to sin. (Sir 15:11-13, 20)

No one who is tested should say, "God is tempting me!" This is because God
is not tempted by any form of evil, nor does he tempt anyone. (Jas 1:13)

Both Ben Sira and James distance God from the cause or source of evil and place the responsibility squarely on the individual person. Human desire is the source of enticements to sin, and the power to yield or resist rests in our choice:

He created humanity at the beginning,
　and he left them to the power of their choices.
If you choose to,
you will keep the commandments,
　and keep faith out of goodwill.
He has put fire and water before you;
　you can stretch out your hand for whichever you choose.
Life and death are in front of human beings;
　and they will be granted whichever they please. (Sir 15:14-17)

Everyone is tempted by their own cravings; they are lured away and enticed
by them. Once those cravings conceive, they give birth to sin; and when sin
grows up, it gives birth to death. (Jas 1:14-15)

While both sages hold the individual responsible, they also proclaim the hope that sin is not inevitable: God has put the power to do right within the person's grasp, not left him or her a slave to the evil inclination.

Ben Sira's teachings entered the mainstream of Jewish wisdom and informed later generations of sages and rabbis. He was the head of a reputable school in Jerusalem two centuries before the birth of Jesus, and was himself something of a hero of covenant loyalty in an era of growing apostasy. Fragments of the Hebrew text of his book were found among the Dead Sea Scrolls; a more substantial fragment was discovered at Masada. Essenes, and perhaps Zealots, were therefore reading his work before the mid- to late first century CE.[6] Ben Sira was respected by the leaders of rabbinic Judaism, being quoted—often by name—close to a hundred times in the Babylonian and Jerusalem Talmuds, the midrashim, and later rabbinic literature.[7] Despite the fact that his wisdom did not attain canonical status among Jews (in part because of his words devaluing daughters and impugning women in general), he remained a worthy conversation partner for sages and rabbis for centuries to come. Ben Sira was therefore in a strong position to exercise some influence on Jews growing up in the synagogues of Galilee, including Jesus and his brothers.

Jesus would not have needed access to a scroll of Ben Sira to have had access to his wisdom. Indeed, it is more likely that Jesus appropriated what he did of Ben Sira's teaching indirectly by attentively hearing, throughout his youth and early adulthood, the homilies of synagogue teachers who had opportunity to learn and weave the more beneficial aspects of Ben Sira's instruction into their own (probably without making the attribution explicit). James's acquaintance with Ben Sira's wisdom, moreover, would have outpaced his half brother's by virtue of the fact that James relocated to Jerusalem, the hub of Jewish learning, and functioned there as the head of a Jewish sect for three to four decades.

It should not be surprising that neither James nor Jesus directs explicit attention to Ben Sira as a source upon whom they draw, nor that they never recite his thought in the wording Ben Sira himself had used. Ben Sira, despite his immense and obvious debt to the canonical book of Proverbs, actually uses the exact wording of Proverbs in only three half-verses. Otherwise, he borrows and creatively develops material from the larger wisdom tradition, including Proverbs, in his own way and in his own words. On the basis of Ben Sira's example, Richard Bauckham understands the sage's practice to be "to express *as his own wisdom in his own formulation* the wisdom he has gained from his intensive study of the tradition . . . *without simply repeating it.*"[8] Jesus and James, sages in their own right, and probably the synagogue teachers from whom they themselves learned, operated in precisely the same way.

The Wisdom of Solomon and Paul's Letters

Paul was fluent in both Greek and Hebrew, and was fully at home both in Jerusalem, where he spent some formative years, and in the Diaspora environment of his native Tarsus. He was well positioned to be influenced by Jewish literature from beyond the Bible, whether written in Hebrew in Judea (like Ben Sira) or in Greek anywhere in the Roman world. Wisdom of Solomon, a work of Diaspora Judaism, appears to have left a considerable imprint on Paul's thinking—or, at the very least, bears witness to Hellenistic Jewish traditions that left such an imprint.

One of the most striking parallels between the apocryphal and New Testament writings appears in regard to the critique of Gentile religion and practice in Wisdom and in Paul's letter to the Christians in Rome. Both agree that the awesomeness of creation ought to have led people of all nations to perceive and worship the Creator, leaving idolaters without excuse:

> All humans who don't know God are empty-headed by nature. In spite of the good things that can be seen, they were somehow unable to know the one who truly is. Though they were fascinated by what he had made, they were unable to recognize the maker of everything. . . . These people could have perceived something of the one who created all things as they thought about the power and beauty of the things that were created. It is for this reason that they're not without guilt. . . . These persons aren't excused. (Wis 13:1, 5-6, 8)

> God's wrath is being revealed from heaven against all the ungodly behavior and the injustice of human beings who silence the truth with injustice. This is because what is known about God should be plain to them because God made it plain to them. Ever since the creation of the world, God's invisible qualities—God's eternal power and divine nature—have been clearly seen, because they are understood through the things God has made. So humans are without excuse. (Rom 1:18-20)

Paul is stronger on this point even than Wisdom of Solomon, whose author begins to make excuses for Gentiles, saying that the beauty of God's creation distracted them while they were searching for God (Wis 13:7-8); Paul will have none of that.

Worshiping idols, and thus remaining ignorant of the One God, led in turn to the disruption of the social and moral order at every level among the Gentile nations as cause leads to effect:

> Everything becomes a confused mix of blood, murder, theft, and deception. Corruption, breaking one's word, upheaval, false pledges—all these things abound. . . . Adultery and promiscuity abound.
> The worship of nameless idols is the origin of all evil—its cause as well as its result. (Wis 14:25-27)

They traded God's truth for a lie, and they worshipped and served the creation instead of the creator, who is blessed forever. Amen.

That's why God abandoned them to degrading lust. . . . God abandoned them to a defective mind to do inappropriate things. So they were filled with all injustice, wicked behavior, greed, and evil behavior. They are full of jealousy, murder, fighting, deception, and malice. . . . They are without understanding, disloyal, without affection, and without mercy. (Rom 1:25-26, 28-29, 31)

Again, we can see evidence of Paul sharpening the critique of idolatry and its effects: the social and moral chaos, including now the inversion of the proper order within the individual himself or herself (with the "degrading passions" in charge of the will rather than the faculty of reason), is a facet of God's punishment of those persons who have given the honor due God to others. Paul also sharpens human responsibility in this scenario. The Gentiles had sufficient knowledge, and therefore their straying represents intentional rebellion against God: "Though they know God's decision that those who persist in such practices deserve death, they not only keep doing these things but also approve others who practice them" (Rom 1:32).

The existence of parallel material in Wisdom of Solomon does not diminish the force or importance of Romans 1:18-32. On the contrary, the fact that Paul has incorporated this material without comment or critique—even heightening Gentile responsibility for error—suggests that he agreed wholeheartedly with the position articulated in Wisdom up to this point. Paul departs from the earlier Hellenistic Jewish author only, and quite significantly, in going one step further, turning the same critical light that had turned up so much amiss in Gentile practice on Jewish practice as well, leaving no human being in a position of privilege before the impartial Judge of all (Rom 2:1–3:20).[9]

The Apocrypha and Early Christian Theology

One of the important limitations that the Protestant Reformers placed upon the use of the Apocrypha in the church was that these texts ought not to be used to establish doctrine. These Reformers had particularly in mind some Catholic teachings concerning saying Masses on behalf of the dead, accumulating merit in one's treasury of works through charitable deeds and contributions to the church, and the like. Their pronouncement, however, should not obscure the fact that the early church had already found the books of the Apocrypha to be invaluable resources as they worked out some of the most basic and distinctive Christian doctrines, including the incarnation, the person of the Son, and the relations of the persons of the Trinity—doctrines fully accepted by Protestant, Catholic, and Orthodox Christians alike.

As early Christians wrestled with the idea that God had visited them "in the flesh" in the person of Jesus, that somehow the divine Son had walked among them and, after his resurrection from the dead, returned to the Father, they naturally began to inquire into the activity of the Son prior to his incarnation. What was the Son like, and what role did he play in God's dealings with creation, before he was born to Mary and Joseph? These early theologians found an essential resource for their construction of an answer in earlier Jewish speculations about the figure of Wisdom as an eternal being working alongside God in creation. What began as a mere personification of the quality of wisdom in Proverbs 8 took on more and more personality and being in the description of Wisdom in Wisdom of Solomon:

> Wisdom, the skilled fashioner of all things, taught me. . . . She is a breath of God's power and a spotless mirror of God's power to act and an image of God's goodness. Being one, she is capable of all things and, remaining intact in herself, she renews all things and enters into holy souls generation after generation, making them prophets and God's friends. (7:22, 25-27, author's translation)

Of special importance here is the conception of Wisdom as an emanation of God and as that which carries and perfectly represents God's image, character, and power. This is a substantial development of the tradition of Lady Wisdom in Proverbs 8:22-31.

It was precisely *this* language that early Christians like Paul and the anonymous author of the Letter to the Hebrews began to use to talk about the Son in his existence before being born in human likeness:

> The Son is the image of the invisible God,
>> the one who is first over all creation,
>
> Because all things were created by him:
>> both in the heavens and on the earth,
>> the things that are visible and the things that are invisible. . . .
>> all things were created through him and for him.

125

> He existed before all things,
>   and all things are held together in him. (Col 1:15-17)

> In these most recent days, God spoke to us in a Son, whom he made heir of
> all things, through whom he created the ages, who is the radiance of God's
> glory and the exact imprint of God's being, sustaining all things by his power-
> ful word. (Heb 1:2-3, author's trans.)

The figure of Wisdom provides the raw material for Christian reflection
on the Son both in his being (as perfect representation of God's image and an
emanation of God's glory) and in his preincarnate activity (as God's agent in
the act of creation and in the ongoing sustaining of what was created).

Church fathers would continue to return to the same passage from Wisdom as they worked out the relationship of the persons of the Trinity, asking questions, for example, concerning the subordination or equality of the
Father and the Son, concerning whether or not the Father and the Son share
the same essence (as in the line from the Nicene Creed, "of one being with
the Father"), and concerning the "eternal generation" of the Son from the
Father (as in the line, again from the Nicene Creed, "eternally begotten of
the Father"). Identifying the figure of Wisdom with the Son, Quodvultdeus
applies Wisdom 8:1 to the latter. The fact, then, that the Son "reaches in
strength from one corner of the earth to the other, ordering all things well,"
argues for the Son's equality with the Father, displaying the same omnipres-
ence and omnipotence (*On the New Song* 7.1–17). The eternity of the Son is
affirmed by Dionysius of Alexandria on the basis, in part, of identifying the
Son with Wisdom: if the Son is "a pure emanation of the power of God" (Wis
7:25 NRSV), as the "radiance" from God's light (Heb 1:3), the Son and the
Father must share in the same eternal nature (*To Dionysius of Rome* 4). These
same metaphors bespeak the identity of the unity of essence shared by the
Father and the Son, such that they are not two beings, but one. They are not
two beings any more than the radiance of light is an entity distinct and sepa-
rable from the source of light (Ambrose, *On the Christian Faith*, 1.7.48–49;
Gregory of Elvira, *On the Faith* 5; Augustine, *Tractates on the Gospel of John*
20.13; *On the Trinity* 4.20.27). In the words of Fulgentius of Ruspe:

> So as to show that the Son is infinite along with the Father, the sacred Scrip-
> ture was careful to say of wisdom, "It is the reflection of the eternal light, a
> spotless mirror of the majesty of God and an image of his goodness." In this
> testimony are shown the oneness of nature, the distinction of persons, and
> the infinite equality of the Father and the Son.[10]

The writings of the Apocrypha were accepted and celebrated as prophetic testimonies to the incarnation and passion of Jesus alongside the Hebrew Scriptures, adding additional "proofs" to the fact that the peculiar shape of Jesus' messiahship was part of God's foreordained and fore-announced plan. One such testimony is found in Baruch 3:35-37: "This is our God. No other will be compared to him. God discovered every way of knowledge and gave her [i.e., Wisdom] to his child Jacob, to Israel, whom he loved. After this, she [he?] appeared on the earth and lived among humans."

In the Greek text, there is no indication of the gender of the one who "appeared on earth," something supplied in the English translation on the basis of context. This excerpt comes from "Baruch's" hymn about Wisdom, whom God sent to dwell with Israel in the form of the book of the law (Bar 4:1-3; cf. Sir 24:1-23). It is natural, therefore, to read this final sentence as a statement about Wisdom, personified as a female figure in Jewish tradition. Church fathers, however, saw here a prophecy of the incarnation, understanding God (the subject of the immediately preceding verses) to be the one who also "appeared on the earth" (see, e.g., Hilary of Poitiers, *On the Trinity* 4.42; Quodvultdeus, *The Book of Promises and Predictions of God* 3.3, in Voicu 2010, 431–32).[11] Here was a prophecy about not just the coming of a Messiah, but the coming in the flesh of a divine being.

A text in Wisdom of Solomon also attracted considerable attention as a prediction about Jesus, this time specifically regarding his suffering and death. Writing of the way in which living only for this life perverts the minds of human beings, turning them into pleasure-seeking animals for whom might makes right, the author describes their persecution of the righteous person:

> Let's lie in ambush for the one who does what is right. . . . He even boasts that God is his Father.
> Let's see if his words are true. Let's put him to the extreme test and see what happens. If this man who does the right thing is indeed God's Son, then God will assist him. God will rescue him from the hand of those who oppress him. Let's test him by assaulting and torturing him. Then we will know just how good he really is. Let's test his ability to endure pain. Let's condemn him to a disgraceful death: according to him, God should show up to protect him. (Wis 2:12, 16-20)

The author was writing of the persecution of Torah-observant Jews at the hands of apostate Jews, but the description here of the righteous person as God's Son, and the fact that a shameful death is imposed upon this person in connection with this claim, led Christians to read it in light of Jesus' story. Augustine, for example, quotes the passage, saying that "the passion of Christ is most openly prophesied," with the text being a proleptic quotation of the speech of "his impious murderers" (*Civ.* 17.20; see also Origen, *Hom. on Exod.* 6.1; Cyril of Alexandria, *Commentary on the Gospel of John* 11.2; Hilary of Poitiers, *Homilies on the Psalms* 41.12; Augustine, *Expositions on the Psalms* 48.1.11).[12] Texts from the Apocrypha were not read merely as prophecies already fulfilled in Christ, but also as texts speaking reliably and authoritatively concerning God's future interventions. For example, Irenaeus cites Baruch 4:36–5:9 (esp. 5:3) as evidence that God would yet establish a kingdom on earth, against the view that the kingdom of God is a heavenly reality only (*Adv. Haer.* 5.35.1–2).

The Apocrypha and Christian Martyrdom and Witness

Early Christians also found the Apocrypha to offer help as they faced the daily challenges of living in a society that was, at best, unsupportive of their withdrawal from the traditional religions of their neighbors and, at worst, overtly hostile. A very early example of this comes again from the Letter to the Hebrews, written to encourage Christians who had endured significant losses of honor and resources as a result of leaving behind the social networks of non-Christian Jews and Gentiles in order to respond to the divine favor they had encountered through Jesus as Messiah (see, e.g., Heb 10:32-34). Toward the climax of his list of people who had exemplified trust in God and faithfulness toward God, and had been therefore awarded lasting honor and the promise of eternal possessions in God's realm, the author names those who "were tortured and refused to be released so they could gain a better resurrection" (Heb 11:35b). He calls his audience's attention, thus, beyond the narratives of the Jewish Scriptures to the story of Eleazar, the seven brothers, and the mother of the seven, who were tortured to death under Antiochus IV, "refusing to accept release" from the tortures by accepting a mouthful of pork as a sign of their renunciation of their ancestral covenant and its demands on their practice (2 Macc 6:18–7:42). While the widow of Zarephath and the Shunammite woman (1 Kgs 17:17-24; 2 Kgs 4:18-37) "received back their dead by resurrection" (Heb 11:35a), this was merely a resuscitation back into the life of this world, to suffer death again. Those who died for the sake of their commitment to God, however, were empowered to endure by their hope for a resurrection to the better and eternal life of the world to come (see, explicitly, 2 Macc 7:9, 11, 14, 23, 29).

The examples of the martyrs of the Hellenizing Crisis became increasingly important in the early church as the cost of maintaining faithfulness toward Jesus became increasingly higher and as Christians were increasingly made both to witness and to suffer the same gruesome experiences as these earlier martyrs. During the persecution of Christian clergy under the emperor Maximin in 235 CE, Origen of Alexandria turned to the story of these martyrs as he wrote to encourage two young local deacons not to renounce their faith when faced with torture and death. Origen followed the account of the martyrs in 2 Maccabees 6:18–7:42 closely, often quoting passages verbatim from this text, but clearly also knew the version of the story in 4 Maccabees, weaving in images, explanations, and other material from this more fully developed account into his retelling of the martyrdoms and his exhortation to his deacons.[13] Cyprian of Carthage would also turn to this story when encouraging fellow Christians to endure for the sake of the faith during a persecution launched by Valerian in 256 CE (*Exhortation to Martyrdom* 11). The Maccabean martyrs were venerated as Christian saints—indeed, they were the only pre-Christian figures to be granted this signal honor. While some early Christians objected to the practice, influential voices such as Augustine's and Chrysostom's defended these martyrs' right to recognition for having contended so courageously for the sake of God even before Christ had overcome death and conquered its fearsomeness (thus Chrysostom, *Sermon on Eleazar and the Seven Boys* 5; Augustine, *Civ.* 18.36).

Church fathers continued to return to 2 Maccabees 6–7 and 4 Maccabees long after the fires of persecution had been extinguished by the legalization of Christianity and, indeed, its adoption as the state religion of the empire. Chrysostom held up the martyrs as examples of endurance in virtue in the face of the onslaught of the passions, encouraging his Christian audience to "display as much endurance against the irrational passions of anger, desire for money, bodily lust, empty glory, and the like as they showed commitment to their philosophy in their agonies" (*Homily 1 on the Maccabees* 11), "cutting back the excess growth of the flesh's impulses" (*Homily 2 on the Maccabees* 6).[14] A similar theme emerges in a sermon by Gregory of Nazianzus expressly based on 4 Maccabees (*Oration* 15). The stories of the Maccabean martyrs were thus used in support of Paul's exhortation to Christians to contend against the "self with its passions and its desires" (Gal 5:24), the "passions that wage war against your soul" (1 Pet 2:11, author's trans.).[15]

Whatever the place of these books in our canon of Scripture, we owe to them and their authors a significant debt for their contribution to the formulation of central Christian doctrines, to the perseverance of our forebears in the faith who endured torture and death rather than allow the light of their witness to be extinguished, and to the ethical formation of the people of God. The imprint that these texts have left not only on the church during its formative centuries but also on the thought of the earliest leaders of the movement—beginning with Jesus himself—commends them to our study alongside the books of the Jewish canon of Scriptures.

Chapter 8

The Apocrypha and the Christian Canon

Do books like Tobit, Ben Sira, and the rest of the Apocrypha belong in the Christian Old Testament? If not, ought they even to be bound with the books of the Old and the New Testaments? And when we look to Daniel or Esther for God's word to us, ought we to look to the texts as they have been passed down in Hebrew and Aramaic, or as they have been passed down among the early Greek-speaking Jews and Christians? What role ought such books to play in the formation of Christian disciples and communities, and what authority ought to be accorded them? Are they, in the end, best "hidden away" from the average layperson, as the very name "Apocrypha" (from the Greek for "hidden things") suggests? These are questions with which Christians have wrestled since the second century, and which still naturally arise today as we look at the array of Bibles used by various churches and available for individual use.

In this chapter, we will briefly survey how these questions arose, what principal answers have been given, and what principles are at stake in the discussion. Whatever conclusion one draws, one thing is certain: we would not speak today of "the Apocrypha" as a collection of Jewish texts had the church in every age not revered these particular books, and drawn constant inspiration from them, alongside the Jewish texts collected in the Hebrew Bible and above all other Jewish literature beyond the Hebrew Bible and New Testament.

The Formation of the Jewish Canon

Beginning in the late second century CE, Christians began making lists of the books they considered to be canonical, that is, the authoritative texts

131

on the basis of which Christian belief and practice would be adjudicated and other writings evaluated. More often than not, these lists were concerned with determining the acceptable limits of the emerging New Testament. We do not find a comparable practice in Jewish communities until the late first century CE. There are no lists of what books Jews (or different Jewish groups) considered the comprehensive catalog of the sacred Scriptures. Moreover, Jews copied their sacred and other writings on individual scrolls, so we do not have the help of bound volumes (a practice that would become dominant among early Christians) for determining the boundaries of what writings might be considered sacred such as a front and back cover provide.

We do, however, find broader references to the major groupings within a Jewish "canon." Around 132 BCE, Ben Sira's grandson spoke of the sacred books as "the Law and the Prophets and the other books of our ancestors," which suggests three major categories of sacred writings. At about the same time, the author of 2 Maccabees spoke of Judas, on the eve of the decisive battle against Nicanor, encouraging his troops with words from "the Law and the Prophets" (15:9). The author of 4 Maccabees speaks of the martyrs' father teaching them "the Law and the Prophets" (18:10). In the Gospels, we frequently find references to "the Law and the Prophets" as a way of speaking of the whole array of sacred writings (Matt 5:17; 7:12; 22:40), though this is extended in one instance to "the Law from Moses, the Prophets, and the Psalms" (Luke 24:44).

Within the various streams of Judaism, there was a clear consensus regarding the authority of the Torah or Pentateuch (the "Five Books of Moses"), which contained the foundation epic of the Israelite people and the laws that gave Israel its distinctive identity and practice—and, above all, its covenant relationship with the One God. There is also agreement concerning the authority of the Major and the Minor Prophets, which included Isaiah, Jeremiah, Ezekiel, and "the twelve" already in Ben Sira's time (Sir 49:10). Ben Sira also relates episodes from Joshua through 2 Kings, suggesting his knowledge of those books as part of the sacred history of the people (the "Earlier" or "Former Prophets," as these books came to be known in Jewish circles). These texts were received and treated as the "oracles of God" (CEB: "God's revelations") as Paul, for example, reflects (Rom 3:2); and their authority rested on the conviction that the will and the word of the God of Israel were clearly and directly announced therein.

Other texts, however, are already considered authoritative beyond these two bodies of writings. Ben Sira's grandson speaks of "the other books of our ancestors" alongside the books in these two categories.[1] A three-part division of the sacred writings may also be reflected in Luke's recollection of Jesus speaking of "the Law of Moses, the Prophets, and the Psalms." This third part, which would come to be referred to as the "Writings" in Jewish divisions of Scripture, is the least clearly defined during the century around the turn of the era.

The Psalms of David were held on a par with the prophetic literature, and often treated as prophecies themselves, looking ahead to the events transpiring in a later period and thereby legitimating those events as God's unfolding plan. Both the Qumran community and the early Christian movement read the Psalms in this manner, in addition to using them in worship. The elevated authority of these texts is reflected in the way in which appeal is consistently made to them as a means of resolving disagreements and establishing positions. If a practice or position can be shown to be consonant with what is found in the Torah, Prophets, or Psalms, then that practice or position should (in the view of its proponent) merit acceptance by all who look to the Torah, Prophets, and Psalms for divine guidance. Here we find these Scriptures acting as "canon"—that is, as the commonly agreed-upon measuring stick—centuries before the word would be applied to a definitive listing of books. Their authority is also reflected in the fact that they became the basis for commentary, whether Philo on Genesis, Exodus, and the distinctive Jewish laws; or authors from Qumran on Habakkuk, Nahum, and selected psalms.

The same uses can be observed in regard to other books that came to be included within the Hebrew Bible, such as Proverbs and the Historical Books (known as the "earlier prophets"). The conduct of David (with one notorious exception), for example, becomes normative for judging what behaviors are proper in new situations, and is offered as decisive evidence in support of those behaviors (see, e.g., 4 Macc 3:6-18; Mark 2:23-28). It is apparent, however, that there was no single, fixed "canon" of Scripture at the time of Jesus. Affirmations made toward the end of the first century CE concerning the sacredness of Esther and Ecclesiastes, or concerning the lack of holiness clinging to scrolls of Ben Sira and Baruch, attest to ongoing debates about the extent of the emerging Jewish canon.

Within some Jewish groups, the circle of Scripture was drawn quite narrowly. For the Samaritans, the Pentateuch stood head and shoulders above all other books (though this does not necessarily mean that they did not accept the authority of the prophetic literature). Other Jewish groups appear to have had a considerably broader circle of authoritative Scriptures. The authors of the *Testaments of the Twelve Patriarchs* refer to "Books of Enoch" as authoritative and reliable revelation, as does Jesus' half brother Jude (Jude 14-15). The community at Qumran refers to "The Book of Divisions" (that is, *Jubilees*) as an authoritative text that determines community practice alongside the Scriptures accepted by most Jews, and the "Astronomical Book" within *1 Enoch* regulated their celebration of the sacred calendar of Sabbaths and festivals. Fragments of five manuscripts of Tobit, two of Ben Sira, and one of the Letter of Jeremiah were found among the Dead Sea Scrolls, the surviving library of the Qumran community. Psalm 151, in fact, along with several other extracanonical psalms, was found included in the Psalms scroll from that collection. But possession and reading do not imply authority or canonicity. It is noteworthy that no recovered document from the Dead Sea Scrolls recites passages from Tobit or Ben Sira as an authoritative text in the context of establishing some position or practice.

By the end of the first century CE, however, an understanding of a closed body of sacred books was clearly emerging. At about this time, Josephus speaks of a closed list of twenty-two books held to be sacred among the Jews, and speaks of this list as representing a consensus opinion:

> For we have . . . only twenty-two books, which contain the records of all the past times; which are justly believed to be divine. Five belong to Moses, which contain his laws and the traditions of the origin of humankind till Moses' death. . . . The prophets, who were after Moses, wrote down what was done in their times in thirteen books. The remaining four books contain hymns to God, and precepts for the conduct of human life. (*Ag. Ap.* 1.8.38)

At about the same time, the author of 4 Ezra (2 Esd 3–14) refers to twenty-four inspired books that may be read by the "worthy and unworthy" alike (2 Esd 14:45).[2] Such a consensus statement probably does not reflect a recent development, nor the suppression of texts read as Scripture by some Jews but supposedly "excluded" by the rabbis at the close of the first century CE. Rather, it suggests widespread and popular agreement concerning what books stood at the core of the Jewish people's sacred tradition, with only a few titles requiring some discussion and adjudication—notably Esther, Ecclesiastes, and Ben Sira.

Josephus clearly knows of several of the books of the Apocrypha. Indeed, he uses 1 Maccabees extensively as a resource for his own history of the Jewish people. Concerning these books, he writes:

> Our history has indeed been written since Artaxerxes in very precise manner, but hath not been esteemed of the like authority with the former by our forebears, because there has not been an exact succession of prophets since that time. (*Ag. Ap.* 1.8.39)

Josephus reflects here the widespread belief among his contemporary Jews that the classical age of Hebrew religious literature was past, a belief generally expressed in terms of the conviction that the prophetic voice no longer spoke after the rebuilding of the Second Temple was complete (see also, e.g., 1 Macc 4:46; 9:27; 14:41). The rabbinic judgment concerning this literature is also based largely on concerns about the timing of their composition in this postprophetic era: "The book of Ben Sira and all books written from that point on do not defile the hands" (*t. Yadayim* 2.13). This statement uses a rather counterintuitive expression to speak about holiness. The sacred books "defile the hands" insofar as they communicate holiness to the hands that touch them; if a book does *not* "defile the hands," it is an ordinary book.

Growing consensus in regard to a closed canon did not mean, however, that Jews ceased to read, value, even highly esteem other texts. The full passage from 4 Ezra, quoted in part above, reveals this quite powerfully. Ezra is commissioned by God to re-create the authoritative Scriptures lost in the destruction of Jerusalem. He is given a fiery cup, representative of prophetic inspiration, and proceeds to recite the contents of the texts while a group of scribes write down the words:

> Ninety-four scrolls were written in the forty days. Then when the forty days were completed, the Most High said to me, "Make public the ones you wrote first so that the worthy and unworthy may read them. But keep the last seventy so that you may transmit them to the wise among your people. In these are the fountains of understanding, the source of wisdom, and the river of knowledge." (2 Esd 14:44-47)

The author of this text accepts a formal canon of twenty-four books that would be acknowledged by all Jews, but regards seventy other texts as equally inspired, coming from precisely the same fount of inspiration as the canonical books. Such books, however, could not be used to win arguments with Jews from outside the author's circles, since their authority would not be recognized. Thus they were to be read only among "the wise among your people" (2 Esd 14:46).

Granting this to be an exceptional position, we find some evidence even in rabbinic circles for the continuing authority enjoyed by works like Ben Sira, which is cited in rabbinic literature almost one hundred times (sometimes as Scripture, though this might result from a confusion of its contents with those of Proverbs).[3] We also find evidence for ongoing conversations about the canonical status of the more marginal books like Song of Songs, Ecclesiastes, and Esther into the second century (see, e.g., *m. Yadayim* 3.5; *b. Megillah* 7a; *b. Sanhedrin* 100a).[4]

An error that is becoming less common involves the assumption that Jews outside of Palestine, especially Jews centered in Alexandria, held to an "Alexandrian Jewish canon" that was broader than the canon in use in Judea. This assumption generally stems from confusion about the use of the term "Septuagint." In the first instance, this is a label applied to the translation first of the Torah, and then of the Prophets and other sacred books, from Hebrew into Greek for the benefit of Diaspora Jews among whom Hebrew had ceased to be used and known, a process that took place roughly between 250 and 100 BCE. In the second instance, "Septuagint" is a label applied to Christian codices of the Bible, for example the important manuscripts of the fourth and fifth centuries. The contents of the Old Testament in these Christian codices, however, are in no way evidence for the canon of Hellenistic Jews in the first century.[5] Philo of Alexandria (d. 50 CE), for example, never recites passages from the books of the Apocrypha by name, and certainly never as Scripture, though he does so recite many of the books that would come to be affirmed within the rabbinic canon.[6] These books he recites, of course, in their Greek translation (and thus, from the text tradition known as "Septuagint" or "Old Greek").

What is important from the foregoing discussion for the question of the place of the apocryphal books in the Christian canon is that the early church was not in a position to have inherited a closed list of Scriptures from the synagogue as a "given."[7] It certainly inherited a body of sacred Scriptures, and continued to use and to appeal to all (or most) of the books included in the Hebrew Bible, but it did not inherit a closed canon. Indeed, the early church was avidly searching for a larger body of texts in which it saw its own faith, hope, and ethos reflected and supported more fully than in the sacred books of the synagogue alone. It found this not only in the writings of the emerging New Testament but also in Jewish texts that did not enjoy equal esteem with the sacred Scriptures in the Jewish community.

The Apocrypha and the Scriptures of the Early Church

Did Jesus or his earliest followers regard Ben Sira, Wisdom of Solomon, or Tobit, for example, as part of their "Scriptures," part of a "canon" of sacred texts? Neither Jesus nor the writers of the New Testament explicitly raised the issue of the canonicity of these (or other) books, though they do consistently speak of, and explicitly quote from, a body of recognized Scriptures that they can assume to be authoritative for both themselves and their conversation partners (e.g., in the case of Jesus debating with other Jewish teachers) and their readers. They appear to do so, however, only in regard to texts from the Hebrew Scriptures. Moreover, they will often speak of the authority of such texts as deriving ultimately from God or from the text's status as part of "the Writings" ("the Scripture," *hē graphē*). While the books of the Apocrypha have left an unmistakable imprint on the teachings of Jesus and the early church, as we saw in the preceding chapter, no New Testament voice ever recites a passage from one of these books in the same manner as texts from the Hebrew Scriptures, but merely blends the material from the older resource into his own teaching or argumentation without drawing attention to the source.

This suggests, at the very least, that Jesus and the authors of the New Testament did not regard the books of Ben Sira, Tobit, or Wisdom to possess the kind of authority among their conversation partners or readers that would yield the rhetorical payoff that recitation of an accepted authority yields. That is, where a teacher states, "as Scripture says," producing a quotation to support his or her position, he or she expects to harness the audience's regard for the authority of that recited text to make them more amenable to accepting the position or conclusion being advanced on the basis of that text. Jesus, Paul, and others routinely appeal to Deuteronomy, Psalms, Isaiah, and such texts in this way. The fact that they *never once* appeal to Tobit or Ben Sira in this way, while clearly showing the influence of the same, suggests that they themselves valued them, but at a level other than "scripture."[8]

Valuing the apocryphal books alongside Scripture, and even *as* Scripture, is, I believe, a Christian phenomenon. This development probably arose, in part at least, as Christians of the second and third centuries recognized the influence of these books on Jesus and his earliest followers, who gave shape to the Christian movement. If Jesus learned about forgiveness from Ben Sira, Paul learned about idolatry as the source of social chaos from Wisdom, and the author of Hebrews learned about faith from the Maccabean martyrs, then the disciples of these men should all the more sit at the feet of the authors of the apocryphal books and plumb their wisdom, attending to these texts as fully as they attend to the books of the Hebrew canon that likewise instructed the Savior and his apostles. Early Christians soon became aware, however, that the Jewish community did not accept as Scripture all of the books that the church, in some circles at least, valued as Scripture.

One important question in the conversation about the canon of Scripture concerned which text of a particular book was the canonical form of that book—the Greek or the Hebrew. In the late second century, Irenaeus quoted from the additions to Daniel in his book *Against Heresies* (*Haer.* 4.5.2; 4.26.3), showing that he and (he presumed) his readers received these as part of the canonical book of Daniel. Similarly, the early third-century Latin father Hippolytus includes these additions in his commentary on Daniel, regarding them as integral to the text of Daniel. Esther was generally read with the additions. Baruch and Letter of Jeremiah, moreover, were often read as canonical parts of Jeremiah's corpus of works, even by church fathers who otherwise exhibited scruples concerning the Apocrypha (as, e.g., Athanasius in his Thirty-Ninth Festal Letter).[9]

A challenge to this practice came from Julius Africanus, a learned convert to the Christian faith and a sometime resident of Judea during the early third century. He wrote a letter to Origen, the head of a catechetical school in Alexandria, disputing the value of those parts of Daniel that occur in its Greek form, but not the original Hebrew-Aramaic text. Origen, himself a scholar of Hebrew and the Hebrew text tradition of the Scriptures, acknowledged the differences in content not only in regard to Daniel and Esther but also in books like Jeremiah (which is about 12 percent shorter in Greek than in the Hebrew text). He argues, however, that it would be wrong now to alter the reading practices of the Christian church, and perhaps naive to regard the Greek text as the inferior and to expect that the Hebrew text would be pure and free from tampering, all the more as God, in God's providence, had given the Greek version to "those bought with a price, for whom Christ died" (*Ep. Afr.* 4–5).

Origen's own teacher, Clement of Alexandria, appeared to have regarded Wisdom of Solomon and Ben Sira as Scripture, reciting and using them in the same manner as he uses recitations from other books of the Old Testament. Athanasius, Bishop of Alexandria during the middle half of the fourth century, attempted to draw a line of demarcation between the Old Testament proper and such additional texts. In his famous *Festal Letter* of 367 CE, he lists as Old Testament Scripture only those books found in the Hebrew canon, omitting Esther but including Baruch and the Letter of Jeremiah explicitly as parts of the canonical work of the great prophet (*Ep. fest.* 39.4). No doubt he also has the Greek version of Daniel in mind when he names that book. He goes on to say:

> There are other books besides these not indeed included in the Canon, but appointed by the Fathers to be read by those who newly join us, and who wish for instruction in the word of godliness. The Wisdom of Solomon, and the Wisdom of Sirach, and Esther, and Judith, and Tobit, and that which is called the Teaching of the Apostles [i.e., the *Didache*], and the Shepherd [of Hermas]. But the former, my brethren, are included in the Canon, the latter being [merely] read; nor is there in any place a mention of apocryphal writings. (*Ep. fest.* 39.7)

By "apocryphal writings" here, Athanasius means the writings of early Christians ascribed to apostolic figures, such as the *Gospel of Thomas* or the *Acts of Paul and Thecla*, that promote beliefs and practices that were not consonant with the teachings of the larger church.

Exposure to Palestinian Jewish practice made a considerable impact on the great fourth-century father of Western Christianity, Jerome. Jerome spent significant time in Palestine learning Hebrew under the tutelage of a rabbi. He desired that his translation of the Scriptures into Latin, which would come to be known as the Vulgate Bible, should not rely solely upon knowledge of the Greek translations of the Jewish Scriptures, but also on the Hebrew texts. In his prefaces to relevant books, Jerome carefully notes the differences between the Greek and the Hebrew textual tradition, thus alerting readers to the major differences between the two traditions in the books of Daniel, Esther, and Jeremiah. He was in favor of promoting only those books accepted as Scripture by the synagogue as "canonical" books of the Christian Old Testament. Only *these* books—alongside the books of the New Testament, of course—were to be the basis for Christian doctrine and practice. He would designate the books of the Apocrypha as "ecclesiastical," signaling their longstanding value in the Christian church and the propriety of reading them in churches and using them as edifying resources. In this position, Jerome followed the example of Melito of Sardis, who, in the later second century, drew up what is perhaps the earliest Christian listing of the Old Testament. His list corresponds to the contents of the Jewish Scriptures, though Esther is conspicuously absent (see Eusebius, *Hist. eccl.* 4.26.7). Melito presented his list as a fruit of his study in Palestine, "in the very spot where these things were proclaimed and took place."

Two major questions appear to have been: Is the Jewish canon determinative for the Christian canon of the Old Testament, leaving aside the fact that the Christian church already embraces twenty-seven books (i.e., the New Testament) as Scripture that the synagogue did not? Are the rationales advanced by rabbis for the limitations upon the canon sufficient in the context of Christian discourse and interests? Melito and Jerome would answer these questions in the affirmative.

Augustine strongly disagreed with his contemporary Jerome. He named Tobit, Judith, 1 and 2 Maccabees, 1 Esdras, the Wisdom of Ben Sira, and the Wisdom of Solomon (which he also ascribed to Ben Sira) among the books of the Old Testament, making no distinction in their authority or use, following the practice of the majority of Christians in the West, among whom these books had gained "recognition as being authoritative" (*On Christian Doctrine* 2.8.13). Augustine's position was affirmed in the list of books to "be read in the Church under the title of divine Scriptures" drawn up by the bishops gathered at the Third Council of Carthage in 397 CE. The additions to Daniel and Esther were naturally included in the form of each book used in the West.

Despite the promotion of such lists, uniformity of practice was still not to be attained. The three great codices of the Septuagint from the fourth and fifth centuries CE, which attest to the reading practices of the Christian communities that produced and used the same, vary slightly in the books that they include as part of the Old Testament. The fourth-century Codex Sinaiticus includes, beyond the books of the Hebrew Bible, 1 Esdras, Tobit, Judith, 1 and 4 Maccabees, Wisdom of Solomon, and Ben Sira. Codex Vaticanus, also from the fourth century, includes 1 Esdras, Wisdom, Ben Sira, Judith, Tobit, Baruch, and the Letter of Jeremiah. Codex Alexandrinus, from the fifth century, has the widest Old Testament canon, including Baruch; Letter of Jeremiah; Tobit; Judith; 1 Esdras; 1, 2, 3, and 4 Maccabees; Psalm 151; Prayer of Manasseh (within a supplement to the Psalter called "Odes"); Wisdom of Solomon; and Ben Sira. In addition, all three codices preserve the longer versions of Daniel and Esther. It is noteworthy that two of these codices include additional books following the New Testament: Sinaiticus appends the Epistle of Barnabas and Shepherd of Hermas, while Alexandrinus adds 1 and 2 Clement and, according to the table of contents, the Psalms of Solomon.

We should not assume too quickly that these codices represent collections of writings deemed "canonical" by those who copied or used them. Their contents may reflect, rather, the collection of what was deemed useful to have ready and on hand for use by the community, thus including both canonical writings and other texts deemed important. The inclusion of the book of "Odes," which is itself a collection of biblical hymns, parabiblical hymns, and one purely liturgical hymn, suggests interests of usage rather than strict limitation to canonical writings. Nevertheless, the fact that the Apocrypha are interspersed among the other books of the Old Testament weighs in favor of their acceptance as part of the Old Testament in the different communities that produced them (with noteworthy variations).

In the midst of growing acceptance of a broader Old Testament canon, notable Western Christian voices continue to question the authority of the additional Jewish writings used as Scripture by Christians but not by Jews. These include Gregory the Great, John of Damascus, Hugh of St. Victor, Nicolas of Lyra, and even Cardinal Cajetan, famous for his opposition (otherwise) to Martin Luther.[10] Similarly, different positions continued to be voiced in the Eastern church, with Gregory of Nazianzus (d. 390 CE) affirming an Old Testament aligned with the Jewish Scriptures (despite his extensive use of apocryphal books in preaching) and John Chrysostom, his contemporary, affirming Tobit, Judith, Ben Sira, and Wisdom, in addition to the Greek texts of Daniel, Esther, and possibly the additions to Jeremiah. What is *not* questioned at any point throughout this period, however, is the value of the apocryphal books for informing Christians, providing models of piety and faithfulness, and otherwise supplementing the religious and ethical knowledge to be gained from those books accepted universally throughout the Christian church.

The Apocrypha in the Reformation and the Counter-Reformation

The Protestant Reformation brought the question of the status of the Apocrypha once again to the fore in the Western church. This was fueled in large measure by the Reformers' emphasis on the principle of *sola Scriptura*, asserting Scripture (above the rulings of church councils, popes, scholastic theology, and tradition) as the ultimate norm by which Christian doctrine and practice were to be evaluated. Such a position necessitated arriving at a clear position on what constitutes the "Scriptures" and precisely where the limits on this collection are.

No doubt the urgency of arriving at such a position stemmed, in part, from the use made of certain of the apocryphal books to support beliefs and practices that Reformers like Luther found objectionable. Tobit 4:7-11, for example, was used to support the belief that works of mercy contributed to a treasury of merits upon which one could draw in the future (particularly, before the judgment seat of God), and upon which others could potentially draw. Second Maccabees 12:43-45 was used to support the practice of saying prayers and offering Masses on behalf of the dead, so as to secure forgiveness and salvation for those who died with sins on their consciences.

The use of a handful of passages was not the sole reason for removing them from the Old Testament to a section designated "Apocrypha" between the Testaments. Luther was himself well aware of the historical debate within the Catholic Church concerning the role and authority these books should have. Moreover, he moved the entire corpus of Apocrypha to this second level of authority as a class, not merely the books containing the objectionable texts. We should also bear in mind that far more objectionable teachings have been based on texts from the Hebrew Bible or New Testament over the course of church history!

It may come as a surprise to many readers to learn, however, of the moderation exercised by the major Reformers in regard to their treatment of the Apocrypha. While outright rejection of the Apocrypha has, unfortunately, become a defining mark of Protestants, particularly where it is important for Protestants to affirm (and defend) their identity over and against the Roman Catholic Church, the Reformers themselves continued to exhibit high regard for these texts.[11]

Martin Luther exhibited this respect not least of all in the fact that he took the pains to translate them as part of his effort to create a German Bible. He removed them (including the additions to Daniel and Esther) from the Old Testament itself, placing them instead in a separate section between the Testaments where, from a historical point of view, they most belong. In his preface to this new section, he writes: "These are books that, though not esteemed like the holy Scriptures, are still both useful and good to read." He does not esteem all of them to be of equal value, particularly questioning the value of Tobit and 2 Maccabees (which comes as no surprise), but in his shorter prefaces to the individual books he has high praise for several. In regard to Wisdom of Solomon, for example, Luther writes: "There are many good things in it, and it is well worth reading. . . . This book is a good exposition and example of the first commandment . . . and that is the main reason why this book is to be read, so that one may learn to fear and trust God, so that he may help us by his grace."[12] His commendation of 1 Maccabees is even more striking:

> This book is one of those which do not form part of the Hebrew Bible, but its words and discourses are almost as enlightening as those of the other books of holy Scripture. And it would not have been wrong to count it as such, because it is a very necessary and useful book, as witness the prophet Daniel in the 11th chapter.[13]

While Luther is cautious, therefore, to make a distinction between the Old Testament and the Apocrypha when it comes to the establishment of Christian doctrine, he recognizes that the intrinsic value of some of the Apocrypha is almost on a par with the books of the "Hebrew Bible" and, indeed, that knowledge of the former is at times necessary to understand what is written in the canonical texts (in this case, to understand Dan 11). "For this reason," he concludes, "it is useful for us Christians also to read and know it."[14]

The Swiss Reformers were a little less enthusiastic. In the preface to the 1531 Zurich Bible, Ulrich Zwingli affirms that the apocryphal books contain "much that is true and useful, fostering piety of life and edification," but stresses their unequal value for the same, particularly when set against the Hebrew Bible and the New Testament. He compares these latter to a mirror, wherein piety is clearly reflected, and the Apocrypha to water, sometimes clear, sometimes "disturbed and troubled water." He advises the critical use of these books, taking from them what is good and leaving the rest, in accordance with the dictum of Paul: "Examine everything carefully and hang on to what is good" (1 Thess 5:21). The framers of the Zurich Confession (1545) would similarly affirm the Apocrypha as "useful and fruitful" for Christians, as long as the contents are interpreted in line with the canonical Scriptures. John Calvin's stance is essentially the same. In the preface to the Old Testament in the 1546 Geneva Bible, probably authored by him, one reads: "It is true that the Apocrypha is not to be despised, insofar as it contains good and useful teaching." At the same time, he makes a careful distinction between these books and those "given to us by the Holy Spirit," which should "have precedence over what has come from human beings."[15]

The English Reformation followed suit, affirming Jerome's position concerning the canon of the Old Testament. The sixth article of the Thirty-Nine Articles of Religion (article 5 in Thomas Cranmer's original draft of the Forty-Two Articles of Religion) lists the books of the Old and the New

Testaments, then commends the qualified use of the Apocrypha: "The other Books (as Hierome [Jerome] saith) the Church doth read for example of life and instruction of manners; but yet doth it not apply them to establish any doctrine." Readings from the Apocrypha continued to be used, however, in public services of worship in the newly formed Church of England, and all printed Bibles were to include the Apocrypha (though, as in the Luther and Geneva Bibles, as a separate section).

These many statements concerning the status of the Apocrypha in the Protestant churches prompted the Roman Catholic Church to clarify its own position. This happened famously at the Council of Trent. A decree issued on April 8, 1546, affirmed Tobit, Judith, Wisdom, Ben Sira, Baruch (including Letter of Jeremiah), and 1 and 2 Maccabees (along with the longer versions of Daniel and Esther known from the Greek texts) as part of the Old Testament canon. This had been, of course, the majority position within the Catholic Church, and was in fact merely a reaffirmation of an earlier, but less well-known decision, made at the Council of Florence in 1442.[16]

This definitive (re-)affirmation, in turn, provoked less-moderate statements among Protestants in regard to the rejection of these books. Shortly following the Council of Trent, Calvin appears more reserved in his commendation of the Apocrypha: "I am not one of those who want to damn altogether the reading of these books. But put trust in them? That has never been their lot hitherto."[17] The Westminster Confession (1647) no longer explicitly commends the reading of the Apocrypha, as had the sixteenth-century Reformers, focusing more upon the limits of its use and the assignment not merely of a secondary status to these texts, but the ranking of the same alongside any human writing: "The books commonly called the Apocrypha, not being of divine inspiration, are no part of the canon of Scripture; and therefore are of no authority in the church of God, nor to be otherwise approved, or made use of, than other human writings." The framers of the Westminster Confession no doubt expected these works still to be read (and, they insisted, tested against the teachings of the canonical Scriptures as one must test any human writing), but the wholly negative framing of the question may well have contributed to the growing neglect of—even contempt for—the Apocrypha that came to mark many Protestant denominations.

The Westminster Confession also takes up the question of the inspiration of the books of the Apocrypha, observed earlier in Calvin's introduction to the Geneva Bible. This is a doctrine of growing importance in the discussion of the place of the Apocrypha in the Bible. It is presumed that books written under the direction of the Holy Spirit, and only these, should be canonical; it is further presumed that books outside the canon were not written under the direction of the Holy Spirit. This replaces the more ecclesiological approach to canon, inquiring into what texts reflect for the church its faith, its ethos, and its hope, such that the church grants normative authority to this text, but not that text, that dominated earlier Catholic and Orthodox conversations. But the shift is more rhetorical than real, for how can we determine whether or not a text is "inspired" apart from its recognition as such by the universal church?

Nevertheless, long after the Council of Trent, one continues to find strong appreciation for, and even commendation of, the Apocrypha. The 1611 edition of the King James Bible included the Apocrypha, which continued to be the practice for all official editions of the King James Version for twenty years. In the Lutheran tradition, Joachim Morgenweg published the 1708 Hamburg Luther Bible containing the Apocrypha, defending his continuation of the practice thus: "They are appended to the Holy Scriptures of the Old Testament, and provided for Christians to read, because they are very useful for the edification of the people of GOD, and are also *a mirror of divine providence and help, Christian wisdom, good household discipline and wholesome moral teaching,*" despite being "not of direct divine origin, but . . . written by mere human beings."[18] The intrinsic value of these texts is recognized, and deemed sufficient for their continued publication between the Testaments.

In England, editions of the King James Bible began to be published without the Apocrypha by 1631. Bibles printed for churches would continue to include the Apocrypha, since readings from several apocryphal books would be prescribed by the lectionary throughout the year, but this was not necessary in editions intended for personal or household use. This was an innovation instituted not by church authorities but by Bible publishers, for they were able to offer a product that was thereby 20 percent thinner and less expensive.[19] The elimination of the Apocrypha from the covers of the Bible altogether was further urged on theological grounds by the Puritan movement in England, which regarded the Church of England to have remained too close to Rome's position and practice in many areas. The conviction that the Apocrypha were not inspired writings argued, they asserted, against binding them within the same covers as the Old and the New Testaments. This position came to be advanced forcefully by foreign missionary and Bible societies, who argued that the funds they raised were intended for the publication and dissemination of the *Scriptures*, and not additional books.

Bibles without Apocrypha became increasingly common, and, in the wake of ongoing polemics between Catholics and Protestants, many from the latter camp came to embrace complete dissociation from the Apocrypha as a mark of identity. As a result, texts that were uniformly commended as "good and useful" by the Reformers themselves, and which, at worst, were to be treated and tested as any other human writings, came to be neglected almost beyond any other—and often far more ephemeral and far less edifying—human writings.

Eastern Orthodox churches generally receive these books as "deutero-canonical," though the official position remains the affirmation of the wide variety of local views and historic canons regarding their use and authority, allowing ample latitude as long as unity is maintained in all essential matters. In this regard, they continue to follow what was essentially the practice of the pre-Reformation churches, living with debate and ambiguity rather than forcing decisions that might fracture the church further.[20]

The story of this debate, lasting now close to two millennia, testifies first and foremost to the importance of the Apocrypha as a body of Jewish writings valued by the church universal. The debate generally focused on the question of whether or not these texts were of *equal* value with the books adopted by the Jewish community as its body of Scripture, or whether they were to be esteemed at a level just below that of Scripture—but still to be prized and read beyond other nonscriptural writings on account of their intrinsic value as witnesses to piety, moral formation, and God's ongoing care for God's people, as well as on account of their importance for understanding the scriptural texts. The church universal has tolerated, since its inception, a variety of positions in regard to the role and authority these texts would play in local and regional churches (and, now, in various denominations), but the position it has least affirmed is the willful neglect or disparagement of these texts. Irrespective of the question of their canonicity or of the source of their inspiration, they remain eloquent heralds of the God who was never without a witness—and certainly not without a witness in the period between the Testaments.

Notes

Introduction: Why Read the Apocrypha?

1. In some instances, the early church fathers use the term "apocrypha" to label books that Christians ought not to bother to read, but in these instances the term tends to refer to heretical Christian writings falsely ascribed to one or another of Jesus' disciples (hence, "New Testament Apocrypha").
2. Zwingli's preface to his translation of the Apocrypha. See, further, Neuser 1991, 91.

2. The World of the Apocrypha

1. The book of 2 Maccabees may have been written prior to 124 BCE, with 1 Maccabees perhaps being written somewhat later. Neither postdates 63 BCE. See deSilva 2000, 247–48, 268–70.
2. The most important include Polybius's *Histories*, the eleventh book of Appian's *Roman History* (the *Syriake*, or "Syrian Wars"), Livy's *History*, and the *Bibliotheca historica* of Diodorus Siculus.
3. The other two principal successors were Cassander, who secured Greece and Macedonia, and Lysimachus, who took Thrace and Asia Minor.

3. God, the Law, and the Covenant

1. On the martyrs as heroes of the Maccabean Revolution alongside Judas and his family, see van Henten 1997, 243–67, 299–301.

4. The Apocrypha and Jewish Ethics

1. This language is taken from the Thirty-Nine Articles of Religion of the Anglican Church.
2. Tobit's version of the older story of Ahikar provides proof for this claim later, in Tobit's last testament (14:10b-11). Ahikar's own commitment to charity is cited as the cause for his escape from his nephew's plot against him.
3. Levine 1991, 48.
4. See, further, deSilva 2000, 95–156.
5. Centuries later, Seneca would censure such people as investors, not benefactors (*On Benefits* 3.15.4).
6. See Sanders 1983.

7. This is reminiscent of the emphasis on securing enjoyment in this life in Ecclesiastes (see Eccl 3:22; 5:18; 9:9).
8. See deSilva 2000, 183–85.
9. Levine 1992, 17.
10. Enslin and Zeitlin 1972, 14; Harrington 1999, 42; Pfeiffer 1949, 300.
11. John J. Pilch 1992, 126–34, esp. 128; Esler 2001, 64–101, esp. 92–94.
12. Pilch 1992, 130.
13. Levine 1992, 20.

5. The Apocrypha and Jewish Spirituality

1. See deSilva 2000, 113–14, 141–43.
2. This is acknowledged obliquely in the statement that "the three began singing *hymns*, praising and blessing God right there in the furnace" (Pr Azar 28, emphasis added).
3. Skehan and Di Lella 1987, 550–51.
4. The sanctity of tithes and firstfruits is also reflected in Judith 11:11-13. In 1 Maccabees, Judas gathers together the delinquent offerings and tithes (3:49-50), all of which must be consecrated in the Temple, reinforcing the legitimacy of his crusade as a "Holy War," an attempt to regain access to the sanctuary and to resume giving God his due worship and tribute.

6. The Jewish People and the Nations

1. On the importance of circumcision as a marker of identity, see Gen 17:10-14; Exod 12:44, 48; Ezek 32:18-32; 44:6-9; Jdt 14:10.
2. If eating freely with non-Jews was highly problematic, marrying a non-Jew would be exponentially more so. Tobit strongly urges his son to marry a Jewish woman, preferably one from the same tribe; marriage to a non-Jew amounts to "fornication" (Tob 4:12). The story of Esther, in which a Jew could be seen as rather happily married to a Gentile king, might threaten these boundaries, with the result that an addition in the Greek version has Esther confess in prayer: "I detest sharing the bed of this uncircumcised king or indeed of any foreigner" (Add Esth C:26). The heroine despises marriage to any Gentile, no matter what virtues he might possess. In another text from the intertestamental period, *Joseph and Aseneth*, Joseph is willing to marry the daughter of the Egyptian priest only after she becomes a convert to the Jewish religion.
3. For a convenient compilation of Greek and Latin texts witnessing to anti-Judaism in the Hellenistic and Roman periods, see Feldman and Reinhold 1996, 305–96.
4. On Gentile ridicule of Jewish avoidance of pork, see also Josephus, *Ag. Ap.* 2.137; Tacitus, *Hist.* 5.4.2–3; Juvenal, *Sat.* 6.160; 14.98–104; Plutarch, *Table Talk* 5.1 (*Mor.* 669E–F).
5. See Tacitus, *Hist.* 5.4.3; Juvenal, *Sat.* 14.105–106; Plutarch, *Superstition* 8 (*Mor.* 169C).
6. See Josephus, *Ag. Ap.* 2.137; Tacitus, *Hist.* 5.5.2; Juvenal, *Sat.* 14.104.
7. Plato, for example, admitted that, while the idols "are lifeless, the living gods beyond feel well-disposed and favorable" toward the worshipers (*Leg.* 931A). The Latin poet Horace could also make fun of the practice of making idols: "Long ago, I was a tree trunk. The wood wasn't so good, so the artisan thought about whether I'd make a better stool or a statue of Priapus. So now I'm a god, and I scare thieves and birds out of their wits" (*Sat.* 1.8).
8. The Greek philosopher Euhemerus offers a similar explanation for the origins of the cults of the gods. He suggests that the gods worshiped by most people groups were originally hu-

man beings, often kings, who attained exalted status in human memory on account of their great achievements or exceptional beneficence. The rites honoring their memory eventually took the forms of worship common to the Mediterranean world. His views are summarized in Diodorus of Sicily, *Library of History* 6.1.2–8.

9. See, further, deSilva 2002, 165–68.

10. See, e.g., Plato, *Resp.* 617E; *Phaed.* 81C: "The body is a heavy load, my friend, weighty and earthly and visible. Such a soul lugging around this load is weighed down and led back to the visible realm by fear of the invisible."

7. The Apocrypha and the Christian Church

1. See, further, deSilva 2012.

2. Similar limitations on charity are urged by Tobit when instructing his son Tobias: "To everyone who practices righteousness, make donations based on what you have" (Tob 4:7a).

3. The author of Tobit also speaks of giving to the poor as a means of storing up "a valuable treasure for a time of need," since giving alms "rescues a person from death and keeps a person from going down into darkness" (Tob 4:9-10). Because of this, "giving to the poor is better than storing up gold" (12:8).

4. In regard to their teachings concerning giving charity, Ben Sira and Tobit continue to exert a strong influence on the early church (see *Did.* 4.5–6, which uses Sir 3:30; 4:31; *Did.* 1.6, which recites Sir 12:1; and Pol. *Phil* 10.2, which reflects Tob 4:10; 12:9).

5. See, further, deSilva 2000, 183–85.

6. Tobit was also being read in Judea at least a full century before Jesus' birth. Fragments from five different manuscripts were found among the Dead Sea Scrolls, dated from between 100 BCE and 25 CE.

7. For a collection of such quotations, see Schechter 1891; Wright 1999, 41–50.

8. Bauckham 1999, 79, emphasis in original.

9. Interested readers may also wish to compare Wis 12:12; 15:7; Sir 33:10-13 with Paul's defense of God's right to use Pharaoh as God saw fit and, by extension, the non-Christian Jewish majority by sending a "hardening" upon their hearts for an interim period in regard to the gospel (Rom 9:19-24), as well as to compare the anthropology of Wis 9:15 with Paul's view of the physical body as a burden weighing down the soul in 2 Cor 5:1, 4.

10. Translation from Voicu 2010, 101. Full excerpts of the patristic texts referred to above can be found in Voicu 2010, 97–101.

11. See also Cyprian, "To Quirinius, Testimonies against the Jewish Position" 2.6; Tertullian, "Against Praxeas" 16; Lactantius, *Inst.* 7.4.38.

12. These passages may be found in Voicu 2010, 49–52.

13. See deSilva 2009.

14. The text of Chrysostom's three sermons on the Maccabean martyrs can be found in Mayer 2006.

15. Gregory's oration can be found in Vinson 2003.

8. The Apocrypha and the Christian Canon

1. The author of 4 Maccabees informally included some of these other books within the category of "the Prophets" (18:10) since the examples of the lessons drawn therefrom include texts and episodes from Psalms, Proverbs, and Daniel.

2. Readers may be accustomed to thinking of the Old Testament or Hebrew Bible as a collection of thirty-nine books, rather than twenty-two or twenty-four. In the early centuries of this era, the twelve Minor Prophets were counted together as one book, as were Ezra and Nehemiah. The books of Samuel, Kings, and Chronicles were also counted as one book each. It is unclear if Josephus and the author of 4 Ezra held to the same definition of the canon. Josephus might have included Lamentations within Jeremiah and Ruth within Judges; nevertheless, it is also possible that Josephus and 4 Ezra reflect different sides of the ongoing debate concerning the canonicity of Ecclesiastes and Song of Songs.

3. See Schechter 1891.

4. McDonald 2009, 227.

5. This error appears, for example, in Oikonomos 1991, 17. This position was decisively refuted in Sundberg 1964.

6. Beckwith 1985, 384.

7. Stendebach 1991, 34; Sundberg 1964, 129.

8. There is one very important exception to this rule. Jude, Jesus' half brother, recites a passage from the beginning of *1 Enoch* (*1 En.* 1:9; cf. Jude 14-15) as authoritative support for his own argument. This book was authoritative in some circles in Palestine, notably (but not only) among Essene communities.

9. On Baruch as an extension of Jeremiah, see also Irenaeus, *Haer.* 5.35.1–2; Voicu 2010, 438; also Hilary of Poitiers, *On the Trinity* 4.42; Quodvultdeus, *The Book of Promises and Predictions of God* 3.3, in Voicu 2010.

10. Collins 1997a, xxxi–xxxii.

11. Indeed, not *all* Reformers placed these texts on a level below that of "Scripture." Menno Simons and the early Anabaptists retained a very high view of the Apocrypha, quoting them almost as often as books of the Hebrew Bible and with equal authority. The texts concerning the martyrdoms under Antiochus IV (1 Macc 1; 2 Macc 6–7) became especially important for sustaining Anabaptist faith in the face of persecution by both Catholic and Protestant opponents. Anabaptist use of the Apocrypha diminished, it would appear, under pressure from other Protestants and as a result of the increasing publication of Bibles without these texts. For an excellent survey of this subject, see Seiling 2006.

12. Luther's Preface to Wisdom of Solomon, as quoted in Fricke 1991, 49.

13. Luther's Preface to 1 Maccabees, as quoted in Fricke 1991, 54.

14. Ibid.

15. Neuser 1991, 95.

16. Fricke 1991, 57.

17. Neuser 1991, 98.

18. Fricke 1991, 65, emphasis mine.

19. Chadwick 1991, 117–18, 120.

20. Oikonomos 1991, 28–30.

References

Abegg, Martin, Jr., Peter Flint, and Eugene Ulrich. 1999. *The Dead Sea Scrolls Bible: The Oldest Known Bible Translated for the First Time into English.* New York: HarperCollins.

Barclay, John M. G. 1996. *Jews in the Mediterranean Diaspora: From Alexander to Trajan (323 BCE–117 CE).* Edinburgh: T&T Clark.

Bauckham, Richard J. 1999. *James: Wisdom of James, Disciple of Jesus the Sage.* New Testament Readings. London: Routledge.

Beckwith, Roger T. 1985. *The Old Testament Canon of the New Testament Church: And Its Background in Early Judaism.* Grand Rapids: Eerdmans.

Bickerman, Elias J. 1979. *The God of the Maccabees: Studies on the Meaning and Origin of the Maccabean Revolt.* Leiden: Brill.

———. 1988. *The Jews in the Greek Age.* Cambridge, MA: Harvard University Press.

Boumis, Panagiotis J. 2007. "The Canons of the Church Concerning the Canon of the Holy Scripture." *Theologia* 78:545–602.

Chadwick, Owen. 1991. "The Significance of the Deuterocanonical Writings in the Anglican Tradition." In Meurer 1991, 116–28.

Charles, R. H., ed. 1913. *The Apocrypha and Pseudepigrapha of the Old Testament.* 2 vols. Oxford: Oxford University Press.

Charlesworth, J. H., ed. 1983–85. *The Old Testament Pseudepigrapha.* 2 vols. Garden City, NY: Doubleday.

Collins, John J. 1987. *The Apocalyptic Imagination: An Introduction to the Jewish Matrix of Christianity.* New York: Crossroad.

———. 1993. *Daniel: A Commentary on the Book of Daniel.* Hermeneia. Minneapolis: Fortress Press.

———. 1997a. "The Apocryphal/Deuterocanonical Books: A Catholic View." In Kohlenberger 1997, xxxi–xxxiv.

———. 1997b. *Jewish Wisdom in the Hellenistic Age.* Old Testament Library. Louisville: Westminster John Knox Press.

———. 2000. *Between Athens and Jerusalem: Jewish Identity in the Hellenistic Diaspora.* Biblical Resource Series. 2nd ed. Grand Rapids: Eerdmans.

Davies, W. D., and Louis Finkelstein, eds. 1989. *The Cambridge History of Judaism.* Vol. 2, *The Hellenistic Age.* Cambridge: Cambridge University Press.

Delcor, Mathias. 1989. "The Apocrypha and Pseudepigrapha of the Hellenistic Period." In Davies and Finkelstein 1989, 409–503.

deSilva, David A. 1998. *4 Maccabees.* Guides to the Apocrypha and Pseudepigrapha Series. Sheffield: Sheffield Academic Press.

———. 2000. *Honor, Patronage, Kinship and Purity: Unlocking New Testament Culture.* Downers Grove, IL: InterVarsity Press.

_____. 2002. *Introducing the Apocrypha: Message, Context, and Significance*. Grand Rapids: Baker.

_____. 2009. "An Example of How to Die Nobly for Religion: The Influence of 4 Maccabees on Origen's *Exhortatio ad Martyrium*." *Journal of Early Christian Studies* 17:337–55.

_____. 2012. *The Jewish Teachers of Jesus, James, and Jude: What Earliest Christianity Learned from the Apocrypha and Pseudepigrapha*. Oxford: Oxford University Press.

_____. 2013. "Jews in the Diaspora." In *The World of the New Testament: Cultural, Social, and Historical Contexts*, edited by Joel B. Green and Lee M. McDonald. Grand Rapids: Baker.

Dunn, James D. G., and John W. Rogerson, eds. 2003. *Eerdmans Commentary on the Bible*. Grand Rapids: Eerdmans.

Enslin, M., and S. Zeitlin. 1972. *The Book of Judith*. Leiden: Brill.

Esler, Philip. 2001. "'By the Hand of a Woman': Culture, Story, and Theology in the Book of Judith." In *Social-Scientific Models for Interpreting the Bible*, edited by John J. Pilch, 64–101. Leiden: Brill.

Evans, Craig A. 2005. *Ancient Texts for New Testament Studies: A Guide to the Background Literature*. Peabody, MA: Hendrickson.

Evans, Craig A., and Stanley E. Porter, eds. 2000. *Dictionary of New Testament Background*. Downers Grove, IL: InterVarsity.

Feldman, Louis H. 1993. *Jew and Gentile in the Ancient World: Attitudes and Interactions from Alexander to Justinian*. Princeton, N.J.: Princeton University Press.

Feldman, Louis H., and M. Reinhold, eds. 1996. *Jewish Life and Thought among Greeks and Romans*. Minneapolis: Fortress.

Fricke, Klaus D. 1991. "The Apocrypha in the Luther Bible." In Meurer 1991, 46–87.

Goldingay, John E. 1989. *Daniel*. Word Biblical Commentary 30. Waco, TX: Word.

Grabbe, Lester L. 1992. *Judaism from Cyrus to Hadrian*. Vol. 1, *The Persian and Greek Periods*; and vol. 2, *The Roman Period*. Minneapolis: Fortress Press.

Harrington, Daniel J. 1999. *Invitation to the Apocrypha*. Grand Rapids: Eerdmans.

Hayes, John H., and Sara R. Mandell. 1998. *The Jewish People in Classical Antiquity: From Alexander to Bar Kochba*. Louisville: Westminster John Knox Press.

Helyer, Larry R. 2002. *Exploring Jewish Literature of the Second Temple Period: A Guide for New Testament Students*. Downers Grove, IL: InterVarsity Press.

Hengel, Martin. 1974. *Judaism and Hellenism: Studies in Their Encounter in Palestine During the Early Hellenistic Period*. 2 vols. Philadelphia: Fortress Press.

Kohlenberger, John R., III, ed. 1997. *The Parallel Apocrypha*. New York: Oxford University Press.

Kraft, Robert A., and George W. E. Nickelsburg, eds. 1986. *Early Judaism and Its Modern Interpreters*. Philadelphia: Fortress Press; Atlanta: Scholars Press.

Levine, Amy-Jill. 1991. "Tobit: Teaching Jews How to Live in the Diaspora." *Bible Review* 8:42-51, 64.

_____. 1992. "Sacrifice and Salvation: Otherness and Domestication in the Book of Judith." Pp. 17-30 in VanderKam 1992.

Mayer, Wendy, trans. 2006. *St. John Chrysostom: The Cult of the Saints. Select homilies and letters*. Crestwood, N.Y.: St. Vladimir's Seminary Press.

McDonald, Lee M. 2009. *Forgotten Scriptures: The Selection and Rejection of Early Religious Writings*. Louisville: Westminster John Knox Press.

References

McDonald, Lee M., and James A. Sanders, eds. 2002. *The Canon Debate*. Peabody, MA: Hendrickson.

Metzger, Bruce M. 1957. *An Introduction to the Apocrypha*. Oxford: Oxford University Press.

Meurer, Siegfried, ed. 1991. *The Apocrypha in Ecumenical Perspective*. Translated by Paul Ellingworth. UBS Monograph Series. New York: United Bible Societies.

Modrzejewski, Joseph M. 1995. *The Jews of Egypt: From Rameses II to Emperor Hadrian*. Philadelphia: Jewish Publication Society.

Mørkholm, Otto. 1966. *Antiochus IV of Syria*. Copenhagen: Gyldendal.

Neuser, Wilhelm H. 1991. "The Reformed Churches and the Old Testament Apocrypha." In Meurer 1991, 88–115.

Newsome, James D. 1992. *Greeks, Romans, Jews: Currents of Culture and Belief in the New Testament World*. Philadelphia: Trinity Press.

Nicklesburg, George W. E. 2005. *Jewish Literature Between the Bible and the Mishnah*. Minneapolis: Fortress Press.

Oesterley, William O. E. 1935. *An Introduction to the Books of the Apocrypha*. London: SPCK.

Oikonomos, Elias. 1991. "The Significance of the Deuterocanonical Writings in the Orthodox Church." In Meurer 1991, 16–32.

Orlinsky, Harry M. 1974. "The Canonization of the Hebrew Bible and the Exclusion of the Apocrypha." In *Essays in Biblical Culture and Bible Translation*, 227–84. New York: KTAV.

Pfeiffer, Robert H. 1949. *History of New Testament Times: With an Introduction to the Apocrypha*. New York: Harper & Brothers.

Pilch, John J. 1992. "Lying and Deceit in the Letters to the Seven Churches: Perspectives from Cultural Anthropology." *Biblical Theology Bulletin* 22:126–34.

Sanders, Jack T. 1983. *Ben Sira and Demotic Wisdom*. Atlanta: Society of Biblical Literature.

Schechter, Solomon. 1891. "The Quotations from Ecclesiasticus in Rabbinic Literature." *Jewish Quarterly Review* 3:682–706.

Seiling, Jonathan R. 2006. "*Solae (Quae?) Scripturae*: Anabaptists and the Apocrypha." *Mennonite Quarterly Review* 80:5–34.

Silva, Moisés, and Karen H. Jobes. 2000. *Invitation to the Septuagint*. Grand Rapids: Baker.

Skehan, Patrick W., and Alexander A. Di Lella. 1987. *The Wisdom of Ben Sira*. Anchor Yale Bible Commentaries. New York: Doubleday.

Smallwood, E. Mary. 1981. *The Jews Under Roman Rule: From Pompey to Diocletian*. Leiden: Brill.

Stendebach, Franz Josef. 1991. "The Old Testament Canon in the Roman Catholic Church." In Meurer 1991, 33–45.

Stern, Menahem. 1976. "The Period of the Second Temple." In *A History of the Jewish People*, edited by H. H. Ben-Sasson, 185–303. Cambridge, MA: Harvard University Press.

Stone, Michael E., ed. 1984. *Jewish Writings of the Second Temple Period*. Assen: Van Gorcum; Philadelphia: Fortress Press.

Sundberg, Albert C. 1964. *The Old Testament of the Early Church*. Cambridge, MA: Harvard University Press.

Tcherikover, Victor. 1959. *Hellenistic Civilization and the Jews*. Philadelphia: Jewish Publication Society.

VanderKam, James C., ed. 1992. *"No One Spoke Ill of Her": Essays on Judith*. Atlanta: Scholars Press.

van Henten, Jan W. 1997. *The Maccabean Martyrs as Saviours of the Jewish People: A Study of 2 and 4 Maccabees*. Leiden: Brill.

References

Vinson, Martha, trans. 2003. *St. Gregory of Nazianzus: Select Orations*. Washington, D.C.: Catholic University of America Press.

Voicu, Sever J. 2010. *Apocrypha*. Ancient Christian Commentary on Scripture. Old Testament 15. Downers Grove, IL: InterVarsity Press.

Wright, Benjamin G., III. 1999. "Sanhedrin 100b and Rabbinic Knowledge of Ben Sira." In *Treasures of Wisdom: Studies in Ben Sira and the Book of Wisdom; Festschrift M. Gilbert*, edited by Nuria Calduch-Benages and Jacques Vermeylen, 41–50. BETL 143. Leuven: Peeters.